50
Chester Civic Trust
1960 - 2010

PRESERVATION AND PROGRESS

- THE STORY OF CHESTER SINCE 1960

Peter de Figueiredo and Cyril Morris
Edited by Stephen Langtree

The Chester Civic Trust

Published by The Chester Civic Trust
Bishop Lloyd's Palace
51-53 Watergate Row
Chester CH1 2LE

Registered Charity No 504634

First published in the UK in 2012
Copyright © 2012 The Chester Civic Trust

ISBN 978-0-9540152-1-3

Designed by de Winter • www.thinkdewinter.co.uk

*"Nowhere should be without its
civic society and no-one should be without
the voice you can provide"*

HRH THE PRINCE OF WALES

*"The views of civic societies should be heard.
We need a powerful voice speaking out on the
issues that matter and helping the civic movement
become even stronger"*

GRIFF RHYS JONES - PRESIDENT OF CIVIC VOICE

---

*Dedicated to the founder members of
Chester Civic Trust and all those since
who have sustained the cause with
enthusiasm and conviction.*

Contents

His Grace
The Duke of Westminster

KG CB CVO OBE TD CD DL

A s President of Chester Civic Trust for over 30 years I am delighted to write this Foreword to a book which celebrates its Golden Jubilee. Throughout my association with the Trust I have admired the energy and dedication of its members. Theirs is no flight of fancy or passing phase but, in many cases, a life-long commitment to a city we all love.

Compared to some places Chester may seem to have changed little in the past 50 years. The reality is that it changed dramatically in the 1960s and had it not been for the efforts of the Civic Trust much of what we value today might have been lost. Heritage and conservation are now synonymous with Chester, but that does not mean that change has stopped – nor should it. The important thing is that in a place with such amazing townscape 'change' must complement and not detract.

There is nothing wrong with caring for the places where we live and work, nor anything new about 'the big society' – it's what Chester Civic Trust is all about.

Sir Donald Insall CBE

In any successful programme of urban conservation, the most significant contribution is the devoted enthusiasm and energy of local people. This finds expression in the work of their elected political representatives, and even more in the steadfast daily support of the public. In this respect, Chester has been particularly well blessed. Throughout my association with the city since the 1960's, and especially when our team was completing the survey and analysis of the central historic area for the City Council and the Government, followed by a phased and costed Conservation Programme, we have been supported at every turn by the encouragement and activities of Chester Civic Trust.

The influence of this voluntary society has been enormous and consistently evident in shaping the broader public opinion in many vital heritage and conservation issues. When, for example, it was decided to pedestrianise a large area of the commercial and shopping centre, it was the Trust which so effectively celebrated this, raising and sharing the cost of returning the High Cross, until then for many years neglected in a city garden, to its rightful place at the central cross of streets. Whenever it has been helpful to share with local people the development of new proposals, it has again been the Trust which has made this possible, by arranging public lectures and meetings and debates.

I am delighted to commend this further initiative by the Trust, which records a significant period in the development of Chester and the first fifty years of Chester Civic Trust. I hope it will be read by all who love and care for the city; we can all learn from the past, and I hope the experiences and examples shared in this book may also help other towns and their amenity societies to meet the inevitable changes and challenges of the future.

We are fortunate in benefiting so much from the energies of such a lively and active voluntary society as Chester Civic Trust.

INTRODUCTION
Stephen Langtree MBE
Vice President and Chairman of Chester Civic Trust's Jubilee Committee

W elcome to Chester Civic Trust's second major publication. Our first, ten years ago, was the final part of a very successful Millennium Festival '2000 Years of Building' which also coincided with the Trust's 40th anniversary.

This second book is the final part of our Golden Jubilee celebration and is the culmination of an idea first discussed in 2007! Cyril Morris and I, both fully recovered from our involvement in the 'Millennium Book', agreed that the Trust's 50th anniversary in 2010 would be the ideal opportunity to put on record many of the things that have happened over the last half century. It is, after all, an important milestone for any organisation, especially one which has tried to influence the physical changes in a city as special as this one.

Cyril is a founder member of Chester Civic Trust, and in his professional career with Chester City Council he was a leading advocate of the internationally acclaimed conservation programme. Between us we might have written the history of Chester Civic Trust from 1960 to 2010 but, as we all know, there is a bigger story to tell. We are delighted, therefore, that Peter de Figueiredo, a former Conservation Officer for Chester City Council with long-standing associations in the locality, kindly agreed to write "the main narrative" – i.e., his personal account of how Chester has changed since the post-war period when bold and dramatic plans were first being aired.

In amongst the main narrative are forty "insets" highlighting the role of Chester Civic Trust since its formation in 1960. Together they tell the story, in words and pictures, of Chester 'within living memory' and, more specifically, of some notable episodes in the 50-year history of the Civic Trust. Remarkably, the Trust has remained true to its founding principles; whether we have been entirely consistent or as influential as we would like to think will become evident as the story unfolds...

In any event, we sincerely believe that Chester is a better place now than it was in 1960 and we hope that this story of the past 50 years will not only be interesting and informative but will help us all to make the right decisions in the future.

Eastgate Street in the 1960s.

ONE After the war was over

Chester reached the end of the 19th century with its Roman and medieval street pattern largely intact, and the majority of its historic buildings still standing. Despite the construction of a canal through the city centre, and the early arrival of a major railway junction, industrialisation and urban development on the scale of other northern settlements never took hold. The early 20th century brought the motor car and a modest expansion of retailing, offices and light industry. Thus, following the ravages of the Second World War, Chester, like most historic towns, faced a dilemma. Was it to become a modern city with new buildings and progressive institutions, or could its economic future depend on the picturesque appeal of its ancient streets? The debate had been rehearsed 100 years earlier, at the foundation in 1856 of the Chester and North Wales Architectural, Archaeological and Historic Society. In the first issue of the Society's journal an article was printed entitled Street Architecture which raised the banner for conservation and respect for the past:

> '...if Chester is to maintain its far-flung celebrity as one of the 'wonder cities' of England, if the great European and Transatlantic continents are still to fill our hotels, and the not too plenteous coffers of our tradesmen, one course only is open to us. We must preserve inviolate our city's rare attractions...our quaint old Rows... must not be idly sacrificed at Mammon's reckless shrine'.

In 1945 the national mood for change was strong. In part this arose from a need to rebuild war-damaged areas, but there was also a view that a better and more ordered world could be created out of the shattered ruins of conflict. Although damage from enemy action in Chester was slight, like elsewhere, people longed for a secure job, better housing, fresh air, good transport, and a healthy and attractive environment. These aspirations were reflected in the Plan for Redevelopment put forward by the City Engineer and Surveyor, Charles Greenwood in 1945, which had an enormous influence on planning and development over the next 30 years.

In the plan, Greenwood identified two principal defects: the old and overcrowded areas of small and outworn houses, and the acute traffic congestion in the heart of the city. He felt that these matters could only be satisfactorily resolved through a comprehensive programme of works, with wartime upheaval offering a unique opportunity to achieve it. In the report, he made six major recommendations. First on the list was the construction of an outer and inner by-pass; the outer to divert through traffic, and the inner to take local traffic around the shopping centre. Another priority was the clearance of old housing, principally in Newtown and Boughton, allowing scope for large scale re-planning; the displaced residents were to be re-housed on the outskirts. The architectural treatment of new buildings within the City Walls was to conform with existing buildings in spirit and character, and inharmonious buildings were to be opposed. In contrast, he felt that development outside the walls should be more modern in style to emphasise the distinction of the old city from the new. Views of the cathedral were to be opened

Old and overcrowded areas of small and outworn houses.

up from Gorse Stacks and Frodsham Street. Finally he urged that the City Walls should be cleared of buildings and opened up for view along their whole length.

He saw the inner ring road as the most important challenge, and considered a number of alternative routes for the western section between Grosvenor Road and Northgate Street. Significantly, he rejected the route that was ultimately to be constructed on the grounds that it would be too damaging to the City Walls and the fine views it afforded. Instead, he favoured a route that was contained within the walls, despite the fact that it would have involved demolition of much of the 18th century property in King Street, the east side of Northgate Street, and the Blue Bell Inn. His proposal for the southern section would have involved demolishing the Row building adjacent to St Michael's Church as well as all the Georgian houses on the northern side of Pepper Street.

Greenwood's housing strategy condemned 2,500 houses over 100 years old, mostly in the Newtown, Boughton and Francis Street areas, to be replaced at lower densities, with the majority to be provided on the periphery of the city. Some were to be built at Handbridge and Lache, where new sewage systems had already been installed, but the area most favoured by Greenwood was Blacon. Here he foresaw a new community of up to 10.000 people with schools, shops, public buildings and sports facilities, commending the site for its elevated position, which he characterized as 'the most bracing in the district'.

All post war town plans included new civic and cultural centres as the focus of community and public life, and Chester was no exception. Greenwood saw this adding in the public mind 'to the dignity and importance of the work of the local authority' as well as 'leading to the economy and efficiency in the

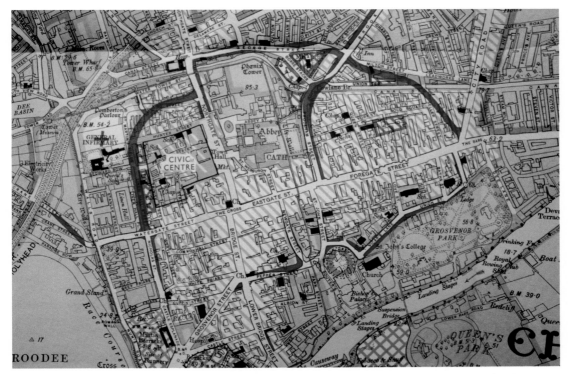

Greenwood's proposal for an inner ring road would have required the demolition of houses in King Street and The Blue Bell in Northgate Street.

administration of the services', sentiments that would sustain little credibility in today's age of political cynicism. The plan included a new art gallery and museum, a concert hall, library, health clinic, police headquarters, council offices, and bus station, all occupying the area behind the Town Hall. The existing Town Hall was to remain for the time being, but he foresaw it being replaced over time with something 'more suitable'. The indicative proposal followed Greenwood's principal of a harmonious style of architecture for buildings within the walls, showing a group of bland Neo-Georgian buildings; though he wisely recommended the appointment of an architect of repute and ability to follow it through.

Greenwood had long been concerned about the state of the city's historic building stock. In 1933, prompted by the Architectural and Archaeological

Society and the correspondence pages of the Chester Chronicle, he made a list of buildings he considered worthy of preservation, which was in turn adopted by the Ministry of Works and published in the Plan for Redevelopment. Yet Greenwood was a pragmatist, and remarked of conservationist opinion:

> *'There is often confusion of thought in the idea that what is old must as a matter of course be worthy of preservation. The real test should be that of architectural value rather than that of age, as future generations will be unable to bear the financial burden of maintaining every old building, and to do so would stultify growth.'*

All in all it was a carefully considered plan. Reflecting the dominant issues of the day, its emphasis was on resolving traffic circulation and restoring civic values, but Greenwood was not oblivious

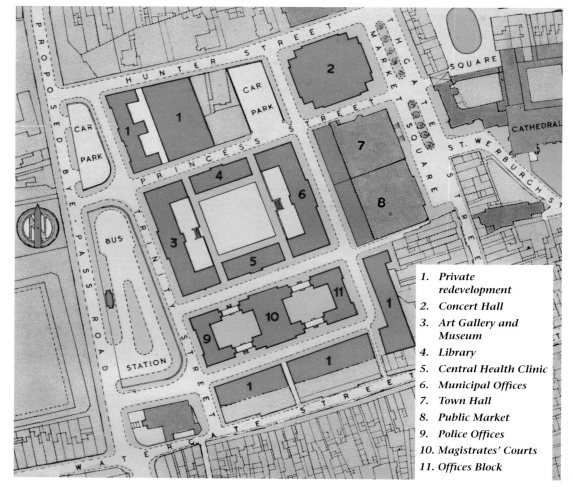

1. Private redevelopment
2. Concert Hall
3. Art Gallery and Museum
4. Library
5. Central Health Clinic
6. Municipal Offices
7. Town Hall
8. Public Market
9. Police Offices
10. Magistrates' Courts
11. Offices Block

Greenwood's Plan for a Civic Centre.

to Chester's special character. In his conclusion he sought a balance:

> *'Chester would no longer be Chester if some of its narrow streets were widened, and its obstructive buildings removed, on the other hand merely to regard the city as a museum piece would be entirely wrong. It is between these two extremes that a compromise has been sought.'*

Many of the recommendations set out in the Plan formed the basis of later decisions, and in its comprehensive approach, it was the first serious attempt to control development for public benefit. In the austere post war economic climate, however, progress remained slow. In common with most small towns, the primary interest of rate-payers was to keep the rates low, which meant there was little support for civic improvements (an attitude that has hampered the city ever since). On the perennial question of whether Chester was to become a dead museum piece or a dynamic city, the reality suggested that neither course was consciously pursued. While in May 1955 the mayor of Chester brashly asserted that 'we are not a lot of old fogies living on our traditions', not only did historic buildings continue to moulder away, but little was done to give the city a modern identity. ■

Aerial perspective of Greenwood's proposed civic centre viewed from the west.

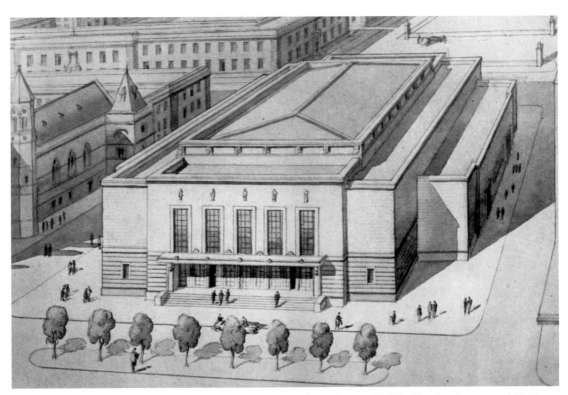

"If Chester is to become a cultural centre it badly needs a large Concert Hall" - Charles Greenwood 1945.

TWO Change and decay

In 1961, Ian Nairn, outspoken architectural critic and connoisseur of townscape, made a visit to Chester, and went away full of enthusiasm. He loved the city's ancient but workaday character, uncorrupted by 'gentility and self-consciousness'. He enjoyed the way that the City Walls were used, not as a coy tourist attraction, but as convenient short cuts; one of the best used being through the back of Woolworths by those en route for the station. For Nairn the Rows had the same appeal, giving choices which for him expressed the difference between democracy and tyranny. He liked the jumbled character of the city's architecture, but also admired the set pieces such as the cathedral, the churches, Harrison's Castle and Grosvenor Bridge, and (with some reservations) the Town Hall. He described the Neo-Baroque Market Hall of 1862 as 'pure Guinness-and-oysters', and in discovering that it was shortly to be demolished for a new civic centre, he urged that the decision makers should exercise great caution.

The Market Hall of 1862.

Indeed his visit was made just as the city was to be challenged by changes more far reaching and rapid than it had seen for generations. The most dramatic was the Forum development which was to cause the loss of the Market Hall, and Nairn was pleased that it had not taken place 10 years earlier, when the result would most likely have followed Greenwood's lifeless vision of polite Neo-Georgian blocks. He also applauded the City Council for holding an architectural competition and selecting a scheme that he regarded as 'not only modern, but sensitive, humane and intricate'. Nairn, however, was an outsider, and for many local people there was a strong view that the Council had notably failed to recognise the city's unique assets when making planning decisions. A satirical article in the October 1960 edition of Cheshire Life entitled

Ian Nairn.

The façade of the Market Hall, described by Ian Nairn as 'pure Guinness-and-oysters'.

'Splendid Example of a Fortified Medieval Town' was illustrated with a series of photos showing city centre buildings in decay, surrounded by litter, graffiti, abandoned vehicles and waste ground. It was against this background, in which the rapidly quickening pace of change posed a major threat to Chester's historic character, that on 7 January 1960 the Chester Civic Trust was born.

Amongst the first issues with which the Trust had to deal were two controversial Council decisions. The first was a resolution to demolish the Blue Bell in Northgate Street, an important building dating from the 15th century with a fine crown post roof. The second was the grant of planning approval for an eight-storey office building on Frodsham Street that would have obscured views of the City Walls and cathedral. These projects came to symbolise the tensions between preservation and progress which were about to intensify, and underlined the need for an informed and independent force that could campaign constructively for sensitive development in a historic context.

Continued on page 22→

City Centre buildings in decay.

1960 In the beginning...

In the second half of 1959 there were informal meetings of people in Chester who were concerned about the major changes which were occurring or about to occur: the Market Hall redevelopment, the Grosvenor-Laing shopping centre and the inner ring road. They were also perturbed about the general disrepair of buildings in the city centre, most evident in Watergate Street and Lower Bridge Street but also including individual buildings such as the Blue Bell in Northgate Street. They were well aware of, and concerned by, what was happening in other towns and cities.

The prime mover was James Chandler. He had been brought up in India and was a former Army officer who had been appointed MBE for his wartime services. He came to live in Chester in 1950 and was head of a business in Ellesmere Port. From his house in Curzon Park he had a panoramic view over the Roodee to the city.

James Chandler's letter, written in November 1959 to a number of prominent

Solicitor Hugh Wickham chaired the public meeting at the Blossoms Hotel on 7th January 1960. A former Sheriff of Chester, he died six days after the Trusts 50th anniversary at the age of 101. He walked to his office every morning with his dog, Judy!

citizens, suggested the formation of an amenity society. The society would temper attachment to the past with recognition of the need for change and demonstrate a positive interest in replanning and rebuilding In Chester. Chandler's letter met with an immediate and enthusiastic response. A public meeting chaired by solicitor Hugh Wickham was held at the Blossoms Hotel on 7th January 1960. The 120 people present agreed to the formation of a society – The Chester Civic Trust was born! An interim committee was elected to draw up a constitution and, in the following month, a further meeting was held at the Blossoms Hotel to approve the constitution and elect an executive council. Advice on the formation of a Civic Trust had been received from the national Civic Trust and Colonel Grosvenor had agreed to become President, thus beginning the association of the Grosvenor family with Chester Civic Trust which has continued for the past fifty years.

Col. F C Saxon OBE MC JP was a Chester architect. He was the first chairman of Chester Civic Trust and a Vice President of the Trust from 1962 to 1973.

James Chandler MBE was the first honorary secretary of Chester Civic Trust; he is seen (right) with Donald Insall in 1972. When He resigned as Vice President in 1974 and went to live abroad, the Trust's Council recorded that "no one did more than he to establish the Trust as a body capable of exercising an influence for good in matters affecting the City's architectural and environmental heritage".

Gertrude Jones JP, better known in the city as Mrs Basil Jones, was chairman of Chester Civic Trust 1966-71, vice chairman 1971-76 and subsequently a Vice President until 1993. Her obituary described her as "one of the legendary figures from the early days of the Trust".

James Chandler's enthusiasm and organising ability had enabled the Trust to be up and running within three months of his letter. As James Latham recalls, Chandler was a passionate advocate of contemporary architecture and design and was distressed at the tendency of the city to approve schemes which were, in his opinion, rather backward looking. Others have recalled more personal aspects of his life; his ownership of one of the first Charles Eames' chairs, his two cats with their baskets at the foot of the stairs and his highly polished shoes!

At the first meeting of the executive council, five standing committees were established.

The first Annual Report also records the meetings held and outings arranged including, in July 1960, the first visit of the Trust to another city – Coventry.

In the following April, 250 people attended the Trust's first public lecture when Ian Nairn was invited to speak in the Town Hall on *New buildings with old – problems in architectural relationships*. The title epitomises the continuing reason for the existence of the Trust and that first lecture is now celebrated by the annual Ian Nairn memorial lecture.

At the close of the first year, membership had reached a total of 322. ∎

London artist, Mr D E Cook, designed the Trust's symbol, which was intended to convey the character of Chester – a walled, Cathedral city.

The Chester Civic Trust

The Blue Bell in Northgate Street was threatened with demolition for road widening.

The crisis over the Blue Bell reached its peak in February 1960, when the Town Clerk wrote to the Minister of Housing and Local Government (MHLG) seeking consent for demolition. The building had been acquired by the City Council in the 1930s for road widening, but had been neglected ever since, with the result that it had fallen into very poor condition, needing £2,500 worth of essential repairs. The Council's case was that even though the line of the proposed ring road had been changed from Greenwood's preferred route, sooner or later Northgate Street would have to be widened and any building jutting into the street would have to go. Thus there was no point in spending a lot of money on it.

The Chester Civic Trust was determined in its opposition, but at the same time wanted to work with, rather than against the Council. Taking advantage of this accommodating approach, the Town Clerk suggested to the Secretary of the Trust, James Chandler, that they might like to raise the necessary funds from the public, a notion that was politely rejected, Chandler pointing out that they could not realistically ask their members and the public to contribute to work which should be the responsibility of the Corporation. According to the Chester Chronicle the issue occasioned more newsprint than anything previous, and in July, feeling bruised, the Council backed down and allocated the funds for repairs, which were duly carried out. Meanwhile, the plans for a tower block in Frodsham Street were quietly dropped. These early wins heralded a significant role for the Trust in an increasing climate of unease about the future of Chester. Functional obsolescence, structural decay and the chronic state of traffic congestion were all conspiring to force a radically different pattern on the city, and the founders of the Trust were well aware that Chester was in for a decade or two of rapid change. ■

1961 'Looking at Chester' - the Trust's first exhibition... and a cautionary tale

Early in 1961 Chester Civic Trust organised an exhibition of photographs in the Town Hall as part of an International Fortnight. It was divided into six sections: Chester and its Waterways, Pedestrian Ways, Levels of the City, Diversity of the architecture, Minutiae and Monumental. Several of the photographs had been taken by Trust members Quentin Hughes and John Makinson. The majority, however, were by Edward Chambré Hardman the noted Liverpool portrait and landscape photographer who opened a Studio at 27 St Werburgh Street, Chester in 1938.

The aim of the exhibition was to encourage the public to look more closely at the details and the often disregarded features of the city. The exhibition catalogue included a commentary on each photograph and concluded *"there is much of interest and satisfaction in Chester for those with an eye to detail"*.

Hardman's evocative black and white photographs are still a significant record of the city, and his house and studio in Rodney Street, Liverpool are now owned by the National Trust. Many of the original photographs from the Chester exhibition have been retained in the Civic Trust's archives and some have been exhibited at Bishop Lloyd's Palace in recent years.

The Civic Trust shared the Town Hall Assembly Room with an exhibition by the City Archivist. Cyril Morris recalls mounting the photographs and titles on the evening before the exhibition was due to open. Having completed 'hanging' the Civic Trust's exhibition he found that the City Archivist, who lodged with his next door neighbour, was a long way from finishing her exhibition and had no assistance. He gallantly stayed on to help but when he left she still had much to do; it transpired later that she worked through the night and had slept for a few hours in her office in the basement of the Town Hall. Cyril also recalls that the following morning his neighbour, realising that her lodger had not returned the previous night, and knowing that he had been engaged in a similar activity at the Town Hall, discreetly (or maybe indiscreetly) enquired of his wife as to whether he had returned home the previous evening! ∎

Photograph and caption from the 1961 exhibition: Castle Street off Lower Bridge Street. Chester has buildings dating from many different centuries and built in as many different styles. The very diversity is in itself an attraction.

THREE

History under siege

The two biggest projects to occupy the Chester Civic Trust in its first year were the Forum, or Central Development Scheme as it was then known, and the inner ring road. In the case of the Forum, relations between the Trust and the City Council were generally cordial, with the Trust enthusiastically supporting the proposal to hold a competition for this huge redevelopment, which was launched in the autumn of 1960. The scheme involved redeveloping an area of 20,000 sq metres to provide an extension of the Town Hall with offices, shops, a theatre and a new market with multi-level car parks. The well-respected architect/planner George Grenfell Baines, founder of Building Design Partnership, was appointed to advise on matters of architecture and civic design relating to the Forum. 24 schemes were submitted, including designs by Richard Seifert and Partners, Erno Goldfinger and Frederick Gibberd, and at a public exhibition in March 1961, it was announced that Grenfell Baines had recommended that the scheme designed by Michael Lyell Associates for the developer Ian Hart

be selected. In his appraisal, Grenfell Baines argued that the human scale of Chester had inspired Lyell's design, which addressed the needs of the city without destroying its character, and the decision by the Council to accept his recommendation was generally welcomed. *Continued on page 28→*

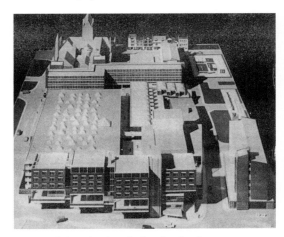

Model of the winning design for the forum development viewed from the inner ring road.

The Forum from the Town Hall Square.

George Grenfell Baines (right) and Sid Tasker (far left), his partner on the Chester consultancy.

1963 Chester Photographic Survey

I n 1916 the idea of 'the camera as historian' was described in a book bearing that title. Although Chester was a much photographed city it was not until 1963, following the formation of Chester Civic Trust, that an awareness of our heritage and the rapidly increasing changes that were taking place led to the formation of the Chester Photographic Survey.

The Survey was launched on 18th November at a meeting held at St John's Cottage, the home of Drs Geoffrey and Rosemary Martin, with the aim, as described by J G McPeake, the City's Librarian at that time, *"preparing a systematic house by house photographic survey of the City of Chester, the area within the walls and buildings in immediate danger of demolition being given priority"*.

It was formally constituted shortly afterwards under the joint auspices of Chester Civic Trust, the Chester Photographic Society

St Martin's Church, Nicholas Street (1959).

and the Library Committee of Chester City Council. John Makinson represented the Trust in their pioneering days, responsible for its basic black and white coverage of the city's housing stock. By 1965 some 4,000

St Martin's Cottages, Nicholas Street (1956).

Clockwise from top left: Northgate Brewery; Griffiths Mill, Canalside; Blue Star Garage, Frodsham Street; King's Head Hotel, Grosvenor Street; Northgate Railway Station and Royalty Theatre, City Road.

photographs of streets and buildings had been taken and all the more important buildings threatened with imminent demolition or alteration had been covered. The Trust has continued to give enthusiastic support to the continuing work of the group's volunteers and the Survey is still supported and administered by the local authority. Whilst the scope of the Survey has widened considerably to provide a social and architectural record, the basic objective is still to record the face of Chester as it is at the moment and to show subsequent alterations and developments with the passage of time.

When the members celebrated 40 years of the Photographic Survey in 2003 with an exhibition appropriately titled *Saved!*

In the click of time, the chairman, Graham Fisher, thanked the volunteers past and present who had helped build up the comprehensive visual record of the city. The work of the Survey continues and it is the role of the Trust's representative to bring to the notice of the Survey team any building or street threatened with demolition or alteration. The current work of the Survey has been supplemented with many old photographs, prints and maps from the Chester Library's local history collection and by notable personal collections such as that by E Gardner Williams. Their intention now is to digitise the collection, which comprises over 14,000 black and white slides, and over 5,000 colour slides, and to make it available on-line. ∎

The Yacht Inn and Nicholas Street looking south in 1964.

Grenfell Baines' view that the Forum scheme represented 'sound and imaginative planning, expressed in good modern architecture', and Ian Nairn's similarly complimentary remarks ring hollow today, considering the harmful impact the scheme has had on the character of the city. Indeed enthusiasm for the project was short-lived – even Nairn was more ambivalent when he returned 10 years later – and when it was partially completed in 1967, the bulky form and brutalist aesthetic of the complex met with a generally hostile reception from local people. The problems, however, can be traced largely to the nature of the brief, which envisaged a megastructure – a single large building – at odds with the grain of the city, inward looking and closed to the public at night. In this large sector of the walled city, the historic street pattern was disregarded, connections were lost, street life was negated, and the needs of the motor car were given precedence over those of the pedestrian. Valuable archaeology too was destroyed. In architectural terms, the bold cantilevers, jutting cliffs of brickwork and broken surfaces gave the massive building a degree of visual excitement, but in scale it related awkwardly to its surroundings, and compared to the much-loved market hall that stood there before, it failed to gain the affection of the citizens of Chester.

Whatever the long term consequences of the Forum development, at the time all parties agreed that Grenfell Baines's professional input had been helpful. For the City Council it provided legitimacy as well as informed advice, while for the Trust it offered an independent agent free of political constraints, with whom they could engage. Following his involvement in the Forum competition, and at the Chester Civic Trust's suggestion, he was asked to advise the Council on the design of the inner ring road and subsequently to prepare a plan for the central area. The Trust came to regard his appointment as consultant architect and planner as one of its most successful achievements.

The development of the Forum was closely linked to the inner ring road. The first stage of this long awaited traffic initiative had commenced with the widening of Little St John Street in 1938, but then, with the outbreak of war, it had stalled. Greenwood's favoured route for the north western section involving the clearance of much of King Street was finally abandoned in 1960, and with government agreement to fund 75 per cent of the construction cost of £1.2 million, the project gained new momentum. The revised plan involved continuing the line of Nicholas Street northwards, breaching the City Wall and crossing the canal on a flyover to a new roundabout at the top of Northgate Street, the option that Greenwood had previously rejected as too damaging. Within the Chester Civic Trust opinion on the scheme was divided. Whilst no-one doubted the need to find a way of relieving the city's traffic congestion as a means of safeguarding Chester's role as a regional centre, the loss of so many historic buildings seemed a heavy price to pay. After much debate, the Trust decided to support the scheme, but when the demolition proposals were submitted to the Ministry of Housing and Local Government, some members broke ranks and objected. An alternative scheme prepared by the architect and

Egerton House, Upper Northgate Street.

former mayor, P H Lawson, for the Ancient Monuments Society, which would have saved Egerton House in Northgate Street together with most of the buildings on Nicholas Street, was disregarded.

In the early 1960s urban planning was much influenced by the government advice manual *The Redevelopment of Central Areas*. This advocated that tightly drawn inner ring roads should give access to car parks around the edge, thus allowing city centres to be freed of traffic, while land should be consolidated into zones by clearing out 'non-conforming uses'. Meanwhile Colin Buchanan's *Traffic in Towns* was the first study to take a serious look at the impending explosion of car ownership and its likely impact. Buchanan predicted that the number of cars on the road would grow from five million in 1960 to 19 million by 1980 and 30 million by 2000, and he believed that roads and

Aerial view of the inner ring road under construction.

car parks would have to be constructed to cope with demand.

With the opening of the Chester inner ring road by Barbara Castle, Minister of Transport, in 1966, traffic flows improved, and after construction of multi-level car parks along its edge, access to the retail centre was facilitated. But 46 years later, the scale of environmental damage that the road caused remains apparent. From the Hoole railway bridge to the Northgate roundabout and the Bars, a shattered townscape of vacant land, exposed back walls of terraced houses and raw edges is the visitor's first view of the city centre. Along Nicholas Street and St Martin's Way, in place of historic buildings, there are car decks and blank frontages. The viaduct and the road line cut across the grain of the city, severing the centre from the inner suburbs and the river, and dividing communities. The idea of driving a dual carriageway through the medieval City Wall now seems preposterous. Yet the solution to bridging the gap in the wall that was created is perhaps the most satisfying aspect of the whole project, for St Martin's Gate, designed by the City Engineer, AHF Jiggens, in association with the Council's consultant

architect, George Grenfell Baines, is a graceful modern structure that makes no claims for attention.

At the time that the Forum was under construction, the Grosvenor Laing development bounded by Eastgate Street, Bridge Street and Pepper Street was also being built. This new retail scheme too was planned to benefit from increased traffic flows. While the Forum took 11 years to complete, the Grosvenor Precinct, designed by the Percy Thomas Partnership, took just two, opening in 1964. *Continued on page 34→*

St Martin's Gate.

Sketch designs for St Martin's Gate and the viaduct below by SH Tasker of Building Design Partnership.

St Martin's Gate.

1963 The Trust P... P... P... Picks up a ...

One of the more bizarre proposals made by Chester Civic Trust was for a penguin pool near Chester Cathedral.

In 1963 the national Civic Trust sponsored a competition and invited entries from civic societies. At the end of the year Chester Civic Trust submitted a scheme for a small garden and penguin pool in the Cathedral precinct. The plans were prepared by James Latham with the co-operation of Chester Zoo and, when the results were announced the following year, Chester Civic Trust was declared the winner of the first prize of £400!

Subsequent opposition from what, at the time, was described as *"various quarters"* held up the execution of the scheme. Later in 1964 it was decided to see whether all concerned would agree to a garden and aviary as a less controversial proposal.
The idea was eventually abandoned but it had brought the Trust to the attention of the national body and the £400 was a welcome addition to the Trust's finances. ∎

1964 Chester Junior Civic Trust

In December 1963 an afternoon programme of Christmas lectures was held at the City High School (now part of Queen's Park High School) and attended by pupils representing several Chester Schools. Speakers included George Grenfell Baines, the City's Consultant Architect, and Philip Dod, a Liverpool architect who was a member of the Council of Chester Civic Trust. Dr Quentin Hughes, who was also one of the speakers, suggested that they should form a junior branch of the Trust and a hundred pupils responded positively to the suggestion. Dr R T Ackroyd, also a member of the Trust Council and one of the sponsors of the younger members' group, promised that arrangements would be made for a meeting of interested young people early in 1964.

John Tweed, a founder member of the Junior Civic Trust and now a Trustee of Chester Civic Trust, recalls the early days...

"Cestrians have a bit of a thing about 'leading the way'. The city's Civic Trust wasn't the first in the country but it was certainly in the vanguard of the civic society movement. Following the Christmas lectures in 1963 and the suggested formation of a junior branch, an inaugural meeting was held in the Grosvenor Hotel with some sixty sixth formers present, mostly from the City Grammar and City High Schools and from the King's and Queen's Schools. Although the Junior Trust was supported by its elder sibling acting in an advisory capacity it was, in fact, largely autonomous and arranged its own programme of activities and social events. Sub-committees were set up for recruitment, development, press, events, and of course 'preservation' (the 'P' word

A youthful John Tweed.

was still fashionable at this time; the more subtle concept of the 'C' word in heritage building activity being somewhat in its infancy). So was born what we believe was the first junior civic society in the country.

There is little doubt that Chester Junior Civic Trust did an enormous amount to cultivate a generation of individuals in the city who developed, in attitude and for many in career, a lifelong interest in the 'Quality of Place'. At this time, from the King's School alone, nine students went on to become architects out of the first two years of CJCT; Pamela Toler, another founding member from the Queen's School, went on to publish with her co-author Gillian Darley, the National Trust Book of the Farm.

Within the first two years of its foundation the junior members helped with the Trust's Tree Survey and with photographic records. They also rescued the sandstone model of the Grosvenor Bridge and developed ideas for enhancing St Peter's Square. There were lectures from Jim Latham on the penguin pool and from Quentin Hughes on Italian architecture. There were trips to the new Liverpool Cathedral and to Castleton as well as a photographic competition, a jumble sale and some memorable dances!

After leaving Chester to study architecture at Manchester University, a decade passed before I eventually returned to work in the City, by which time the Junior Trust had faded. The problem being, of course, that self-perpetuating continuity is very hard to achieve in those transient years when students are quickly moving through 'A' levels and on to higher education".

However, there was another attempt to revive the Junior Civic Trust in the mid-1980s, when Jackie Leech and Eileen Willshaw were prominent in helping a committee of 6th formers from the King's and Queen's Schools to plan events and activities for younger children of primary school age. Activities included a treasure trail around the City Walls and visits to local heritage sites such as Overleigh Cemetery. A newsletter – hand written and hand drawn – was produced and a representative of the committee was invited to attend Civic Trust Council meetings, to give a young person's perspective on Trust issues. Junior members also cleared rubbish and planted trees as part of the Trust's Canal Clean Up Day during Environment Week in 1989. Sadly, like its predecessor, the later Junior Trust also declined as sixth formers left for university and were not replaced. ■

Taking the treasure trail!

Jackie Leech (left), chairman of Chester Civic Trust and Eileen Willshaw (right) explain the junior treasure trail to young people taking part in an event around the City Walls in 1986.

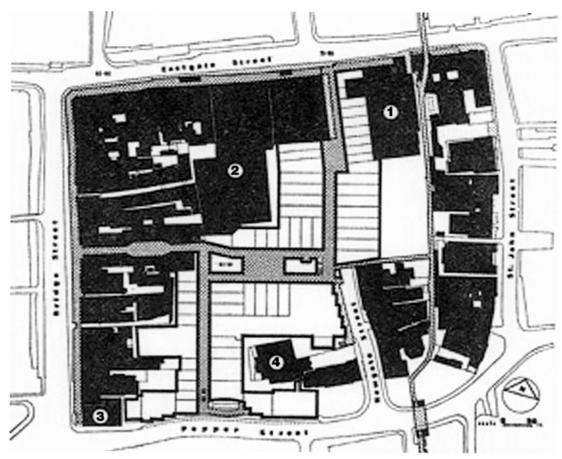

Grosvenor-Laing Precinct – plan at shopping level. The new development (white) is integrated with the existing Rows. Key: 1 Grosvenor Hotel: 2 Browns of Chester: 3 St Michael's Church 4: St Andrew's Church.

The Grosvenor-Laing Precinct – Multi-storey Car Park.

Aerial view showing the roof top car park.

Pepper Street prior to widening for the inner ring road.

Work in progress on the Grosvenor - Laing Precinct.

Although the Precinct caused little visible change when viewed from Eastgate Street and Bridge Street, where it was skillfully integrated with the existing Rows, in the area behind the frontages there was considerable destruction of historic fabric. Unlike the Forum, the construction programme gave no time even for archaeological recording, and the scale of loss of Roman and medieval remains has never been properly assessed. While the bulky character of the development with its towering multi storey car park is all too visible from the City Walls, the scheme was forward-looking for its time, and writing at its opening in October 1965, Chandler applauded the planning concept which separated motorists and pedestrians, and created a tight-packed intricacy in keeping with Chester's traditions. All the same, the Chester Civic Trust was concerned about the reliance on retailing, and forseeing some of the

Grosvenor Centre - façade.

future problems that would come to afflict the city centre, Chandler expressed disappointment with the absence of living accommodation, 'not even a pub', and remarked on its deadening effect on Chester by night. ∎

From the start, the Chester Civic Trust championed contemporary architecture, but always with the proviso that it should be of high quality and related in scale and character to its surroundings. The so-called 'Gap Site', 61-65 Watergate Street was an example of this approach. The City Council had purchased the site in 1938 with the aim of preserving the medieval Row buildings in response to public pressure, but had subsequently, just like the previous owner, done nothing to halt their decline. By 1955 they had deteriorated to such an extent that they were thought to be beyond repair and were duly demolished. In 1961 the Trust was asked for its views on an architectural competition for a replacement building, to which Chandler responded:

'Sham antique elevations should be avoided. A nondescript compromise between traditional and modern is also undesirable. The site asks for a truly traditional treatment – a lively building completely in the style of our own time, to add to the existing jumble of styles'.

The interesting use of the term 'traditional' in this context caused some confusion at the Town Hall, but what the Trust meant was keeping in scale, but using a style and materials of the present time. The competition went ahead in 1963, and from 63 entries, the design of architects Rowse and Harker of Liverpool was selected, again on the advice of Grenfell Baines. When the scheme was published in the Chester Chronicle, there was controversy, and even the

61-65 Watergate Street 'Gap Site'.

executive council of the Trust was split in its opinion about the first placed design. Chandler, however, in his usual measured way, won them round, writing to the editor of the newspaper:

> 'There are certainly among the Trust's members those who are still doubtful about accepting, even in principle, radically modern buildings in 'historic Chester'. But I believe such members will eventually come to see that they need have no misgivings… Opposition to aesthetic innovation is of course no new thing, but history has again and again proved the diehards in these matters to have been wrong…keep history going – build honestly in the style of the times.'

Originally the scheme was intended to be privately funded, but when tendered it proved to be commercially unviable. Courageously, and with government consent, the City Council decided to redevelop the site itself, changing the use of the two top floors from offices

to residential, and in 1968 the scheme was eventually completed. With its board-marked concrete and horizontal windows, it was a product of its time, but the sympathetic proportions, subtle stepping down of the facades, and honest use of simple materials make it one of the most successful 20th century buildings in Chester, and contrasts with the more timid approach that later became the norm.

Continued on page 41→

Implementation of the winning design did not achieve the high standard expected by the Civic Trust. 50 years on repairs are required.

Competition Scheme.

As built.

1964 The Bridge Street Improvement Scheme

In 1964, as the redecoration of Bridge Street was nearing completion, the editor of the Chester Chronicle, Herbert Hughes, wrote of the anticipation of *"The Duke of Westminster 'reopening' Bridge Street, resplendent in its rainbow jacket which might dazzle even the famous Westminster colours."*

Looking down from the Rows, Cyril Morris recalls the scene on 1st July 1964 when the Mayor, Alderman Miss Mary Heaney, invited the Duke to cut a tape stretched across the street. Traffic had been banished from Bridge Street and pedestrians were free to enjoy the brilliant spectacle. They lined the street and crowded the Rows. Civic leaders, traders and others concerned with the project took up vantage points in the street. At a reception in the Town Hall which followed, His Grace said: *"Let this be the beginning of the renaissance of Chester. Let us go forward with other such schemes to make this beautiful city more beautiful."*

In 1962 members of Chester Civic Trust had seen details of the successful Street Improvement Scheme which had been carried out in Norwich, sponsored by the national Civic Trust. Impressed by the scheme, Chester Civic Trust proposed to the City Council that a similar scheme would benefit Bridge Street.

The proposal was agreed by the Council and in January 1963 a Joint Promotion Committee, consisting of representatives of the City Council's Improvement Committee, the Chamber of Trade and Chester Civic Trust was formed. The City Council agreed to appoint a co-ordinating architect, Dr J Quentin Hughes, provided that the scheme proceeded and that at least 75 per cent of the occupiers on the frontage of Bridge Street agreed to take part.

Work in progress: John Welsby (left) and Gerald Burkinshaw, town clerk (right) with three of the sector architects, James Latham, Peter Shobbrook, and John Topping.

1964 Bridge Street Improvement Scheme.

A meeting was held in the Town Hall and a film of similar schemes which had been carried out was shown. There was also an exhibition with preliminary sketches by Quentin Hughes showing what might be achieved in Bridge Street.

The presentation met with a positive response from traders. It was agreed that the street would be divided into four sectors comprising groups of properties. This would give economies by group tendering for the redecoration, the saving from which would help to pay for any alterations to signs or lettering and for the individual architects which each sector would appoint. The City Council accepted responsibility for the proposals made by the co-ordinating architect for tidying-up the street furniture and traffic signs and also for the improvement of the street lighting, including the floodlighting of St Peter's and St Michael's churches.

Following the meeting four sector architects were appointed by the traders, James Latham (Douglas Minshull & Co.), John Topping (Biggins & Associates), Peter Shobbrook (Coppack & Partners) and J Vernon Smith (Saxon, Smith and Partners). Each sector architect was responsible for a quarter of the street and the detailed design of colour schemes within the Rows and the shop fronts below. Above the Row to the skyline was the province of the co-ordinating architect, who also approved the sector schemes.

In a special supplement to the Chester Chronicle, whose offices and printing works were in Bridge Street, Peter Shobbrook explained the aims of the Sector architects:

"We have tried to keep to certain traditions. For example, butchers traditionally have red signboards. This has been revived. The Victoria Hotel, which previously had 'butchers' colours and which tended to merge with St Peter's Church, now had an

Tide of life has flowed strongly in this famous street for a thousand years.

1964 Bridge Street Improvement Scheme Opening.

attractive blue sign. We consciously set out to use shades of grey on the fronts rather than pastel shades which tend to fade."
Quentin Hughes was full of praise for the traders and, in particular, their chairman John Welsby and secretary Piers Dutton (a founder member of Chester Civic Trust). It was, Quentin Hughes said, an attempt to *"pull the city up"*. Chester, he added, *"had been going downhill and looking awfully tatty".*

Because of the variety of architectural styles and the distinctive feature of the Rows, the scheme was more complex and more challenging than any of those undertaken in other towns. Traces of Quentin Hughes' co-ordinating influence remain; one of the most significant features he achieved was painting the Row railings white, giving a visual continuity to the street whilst retaining the individuality of the buildings.

Looking to the future, Quentin Hughes expressed the hope that the traders would preserve and secure all that had been gained and that *"the splendour of Bridge Street would next arouse a competitive ardour in the traders of Eastgate Street"*. The Eastgate Street scheme followed in 1966 and was officially 'opened' by Lord Kennet. Chester Civic Trust was then asked to advise the organisers of a repainting scheme for Northgate Street and St Werburgh Street.

Nearly fifty years later it is difficult to imagine that such a high degree of co-operation with traders could be achieved. Gone from Bridge Street are most of the locally owned shops and cafes of the 1960s. The last butchers, G Venables and Sons, still with their red signboard, will have closed by the time this book is published.

Chester Civic Trust continues to campaign for higher quality of shopfronts, fascias, hanging signs and lighting, all of which would make a significant improvement to Bridge Street and the city centre in general. ■

In 1964 the City Council commissioned Grenfell Baines to prepare a Central Area Plan for the city. It was intended to guide development of the city centre over a 20 year period, and in the preface Grenfell Baines made clear that the Council would need to acquire substantial areas of land. Like Greenwood's Plan of 1945 there was an emphasis on traffic circulation, with a reliance on the inner ring road to resolve the issue of congestion. But in the new city centre plan, the start of an integrated approach to transport can be seen in such measures as one way systems to discourage through traffic, priority for buses, and pedestrianisation of the Town Hall Square. Grenfell Baines also proposed increasing the housing density in the city centre by developing backland sites to create distinct communities in 'urban rooms'. He noted that Chester's share of local retail had fallen in regional terms between 1950 and 1961, and regarded the lack of parking and the constrained road network as factors that would continue to limit the capacity to increase market share; but he warned against over development of shopping which he felt could lead to vacancy of properties and a consequent spiral of decay (which was already taking place in Watergate Street at the time).

Considering the city's aesthetic appeal Grenfell Baines coined the phrase 'Chester's face is her fortune' and cautioned that without its unique environment, the high volume of retail trade per head of population would disappear. In this respect he worried that the trend towards national multiples was eroding the distinctiveness of the retail offer. Noting that there was little to be had in the shops which could not be bought elsewhere, he recommended that the Council should sponsor small-scale 'special' shops at low rentals, suggesting that the upper floors of Watergate Street might be used for artists' and craft studios, or home baking directed by the local education authority with shops selling their work in the premises below.

Yet in spite of these cautionary remarks, the plan proposed a series of ambitious interventions in many defined development areas. The canalside area west of Northgate Street, Gorse Stacks, and the area east of Frodsham Street were to be wholly redeveloped, as well as the areas to each side of Godstall Lane. Several tall buildings were proposed on the periphery, including one placed opposite, and in deliberate contrast to the Bluecoat School in Northgate Street. In Foregate Street Grenfell Baines proposed a multi-storey car park on the site of Parker's Buildings, linked by a pedestrian bridge to a new shopping centre on the south side of the street. Although he dismissed the idea of segregating traffic and pedestrians by building bridges to connect the Rows, noting that more retail activity took place at street level than at Row level, he was enthusiastic about an idea that had previously, and rather surprisingly, been put forward by the Civic Trust for a bridge at the southern end of Bridge Street. This, he suggested, might be used as a restaurant, largely glazed, where he felt it might mitigate the 'explosion' caused by the recent road widening at the junction with Pepper Street.

The design of the inner ring road was not part of Grenfell Baines' brief, but he was conscious of the need to avoid severing links between the city centre and the river, Grosvenor Park and Lower Bridge Street, and made a number of recommendations for connecting the road effectively with the areas to each side. He also worried about the contrasts of scale that the ring road would introduce, and suggested

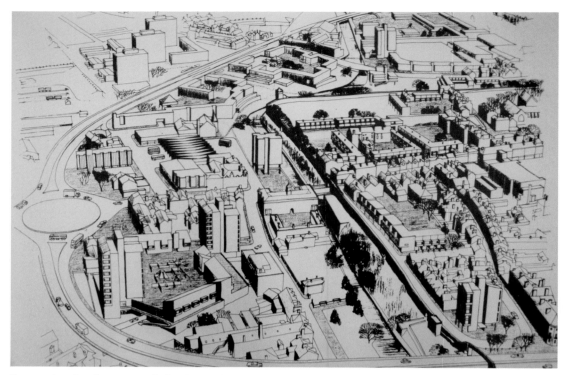

Perspective showing proposals for the north west of the city between the city walls and the inner ring road.

flanking it by moderately tall domestic buildings that would bring enclosure and a human scale, recommendations that were regrettably ignored.

He likened development at the core of the city to filling a few decayed teeth, rather than taking out a whole mouthful, good and bad. His proposal for civilising the Town Hall Square, however, was bold and visionary. He saw it as the principal public space of the city and recommended removing all traffic except buses, paving it from side to side and furnishing it with fountains, seats and sculpture. His vision also involved uniting the Cathedral and the town by removing the railings along the edge of St Werburgh Street, which he regarded as an undesirable symbol of division, and paving right up to the foot of the cathedral walls. It was to be a long time before either of these proposals was to be taken up. His similarly far-sighted suggestion for a Chester University

Quarter, was turned down by the University Grants Committee in 1970.

On the subject of architecture, Grenfell Baines commended historic reconstruction, provided that it was

Proposals for the Town Hall Square.

The model of the city centre, proposed by Grenfell Baines, was made in removable sections so that planning proposals could be substituted and viewed and photographed through a modelscope: it proved to be an invaluable aid for planning officers and councillors.

done well, but also actively encouraged contemporary design. For fellow architects he offered two pieces of advice: where redevelopment involves several small plots, new buildings must respond to the established scale of the street so that existing rhythms are not disturbed; and in

addition to brick and timber, he suggested using concrete, either board-marked from the shuttering or exposing suitable aggregate. To reinforce the point, he added that it was best to stick to a limited palette, and never use multi-coloured tiles, mosaic or faience, which are foreign to Chester.

When the plan was published in December 1964, the Chester Civic Trust offered both the City Council and Grenfell Baines their warmest congratulations, calling it both practical and imaginative. They particularly supported the proposals for living in the city, and agreed that there should not be over-provision of shops. They also wanted a number of immediate actions to be taken, including the preparation of a set of guiding principles for architects and shopfitters working in the city, and a legal framework for protecting unscheduled buildings in the four main streets.

Grenfell Baines proposed removing the railings in St Werburgh Street: the illustration from his report shows (above) the street in 1964 and (below) a montage showing the same view with the railings removed and paving up to the walls of the cathedral.

Such guidelines were indeed urgently required, for just at this time the city was being bombarded with a multitude of insensitive development schemes. There was also a sense that the City Council was deliberately avoiding public debate. In February 1965, the Trust asked if the plans for a new office block next to the Odeon on Hunter Street might be released

Commerce House.

had already been seen and approved, so there was no need to sound out local and national views. The result of this decision was Commerce House.

The Police Headquarters on Grosvenor Road was approved in similar circumstances. In December 1964, Chandler wrote to a national newspaper stating that the public in Chester had not had an opportunity to comment on the scheme until after the approvals had been given by both the County and City authorities. The Royal Fine Art Commission, which should have been consulted by the Home Office, took the unusual step of asking the two Councils to reconsider. After sending a distinguished delegation consisting of Geoffrey Jellicoe, the landscape designer, the artist John Piper and J M Richards, former editor of the Architectural Review, to view the site, the Commission suggested a less formal layout, with the new building closer to the roundabout and no higher than the

to the public and to the Royal Fine Art Commission to allow for comments to be taken into account before the final scheme was fixed. On the instruction of the Improvement Committee, the Town Clerk replied that the detailed plans

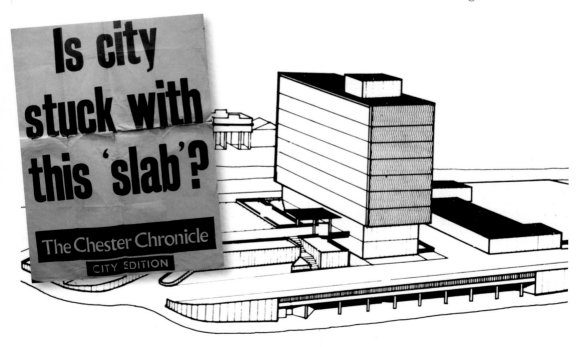

Police HQ and newspaper poster.

Clemences restaurant, Northgate Street.

The development which replaced Clemences. In recent years the façade has been remodelled: additional glazing has been inserted at first floor level and the frame painted white.

surrounding properties, but they were told the work was too far advanced for any changes to be made. The matter was reported by the Architects' Journal which printed a letter from Edgar Taberner, the County Architect, who claimed in dictatorial fashion that '…until the Chester City Council and Cheshire Police Authority had approved the scheme no details of the project could be made public'; to which Chandler, in a follow-up letter to the journal sardonically commented that 'members of the City Council found themselves at the centre of a national controversy over a building which they had approved without (unless they were members of the Improvement Committee) having any idea of what they were doing'.

The high-handed attitude of the authorities and the lack of adequate consultation was a point of principle that the Chester Civic Trust deplored, and in a third case, that of a new building to replace Clemences in Northgate Street, they decided to take matters into their own hands. In spite of approval having been granted before the Trust was permitted to see the Clemences scheme, Chandler insisted on a meeting with the developer, the architect and the City Council. The architect, Harry Fairhurst, however, refused to make any changes, and in spite of the Trust's concerns, no concessions were granted. When the building was completed in July 1964, Chandler wrote to the Chester Chronicle describing it as a bad building, and issuing a detailed and damning critique of Fairhurst's design. Grenfell Baines, who had advised the Council that the design was acceptable, countered with a long letter in which he urged against aesthetic censorship, which he felt would be counterproductive. But Chandler's overriding concern was that the difficulties of fitting modern buildings into the traditional Chester scene would only be overcome if these issues were widely and frankly discussed, and in an attack on the Council's unwillingness to consult with interested parties he asked rhetorically 'can we do without a properly informed, vocal public opinion?'

In the mid 1960s, development schemes for the city centre were emerging at a prodigious rate. Amongst the most ill-judged was a proposal for an extension to County Hall drawn up in 1966. It would have involved wholesale clearance of all the buildings on the northern side of Shipgate Street, where the County Council had been busily buying up properties and allowing them to fall into disrepair. The scheme, which was designed by the

Tom Hancock's sketch of a 'low tower block' which he thought would be "unacceptable and out of scale".

London architect, Tom Hancock, involved new offices and car parking including what was termed 'a low tower block'. Stimulated by the Police HQ controversy, the Chester Civic Trust forecast 'A battle royal with the gloves off', and to promote their case that the area should be developed for housing as proposed in Grenfell Baines' Central Area Plan, a group of architect members prepared an alternative scheme. This showed the majority of the existing buildings being retained with sensitively designed infill development, the drawings being duly published in the Chester Chronicle. In this case the Royal Fine Art Commission saw the County Council's proposals in time and stated firmly that the existing buildings in Shipgate Street should be restored with sympathetic infilling, a course of action the County sensibly decided to follow. At the same time, however, it transpired that the County Council was progressing an alternative and even more grandiose civic precinct on the western side of County Hall also designed by Hancock. This comprised an office building on the open land adjoining the Castle Mound and a glazed block spanning Grosvenor Road in the manner of a motorway service station, which it was claimed would provide the missing gateway through the city wall. Opinion was divided on the merits of this bold scheme, the Civic Trust questioning

Sketch by Tom Hancock for an alternative proposal spanning Grosvenor Road.

Model of Tom Hancock's proposed building spanning Grosvenor Road and linking the Castle with the Police Headquarters which was nearing completion in 1966.

whether it would be appropriate to make such a grand civic statement in a city the size of Chester. On seeing the plans, the Chairman of the City Council's Improvement Committee immediately took sides and declared the scheme to be 'totally unacceptable and unsuitable', which led the Chester Chronicle to declare that the 'Castle Precinct plan may be doomed'. Even amongst County Councillors, feelings ran high, Lt Commander Bruce Butcher likening the bridge building to 'an elevated fish tank' and Harold Weate taking a side swipe at the Police HQ, which was then nearing completion, describing it as 'that ulcer on the body politic of Chester'. When the RFAC was consulted, it came out firmly against

these proposals too, after which the scheme was quietly buried.

Another scheme in the Bridgegate area put forward around the same time involved removing all the buildings between Oddfellows Hall and the Old King's Head to make way for an eight storey development comprising a cinema and a 60 bedroom motel designed by Peter Kilby of Southampton. In this

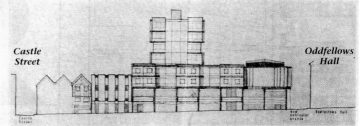

Lower Bridge Street - Kilby Scheme.

case the Chester Civic Trust did not need to campaign, for Jiggens, the City Engineer, opposed it on grounds of over-development, whilst Grenfell Baines felt that a second tall block close to the Police HQ would 'kill the effect of the one already approved'. But in other instances the Trust felt beleaguered. In October 1963, dismayed by the squalid state of the riverside between Grosvenor Bridge and Dee Lane, Chandler wrote to the Town Clerk suggesting that the city's consultant architect be asked to prepare an up-to-date plan for the area. The Town Clerk's response was that the 'time was not ripe for development of the river frontage', yet only a few months later the Trust discovered from inside sources that the City Council was planning to widen the Groves to accommodate more traffic. When the County Council purchased St Bridget's Burial Ground in 1964 for work connected with the ring road, the Trust urged that Thomas Harrison's grave should be re-sited and displayed, a request which was summarily rejected. The memorial stone was subsequently lost.

During this turbulent period there was no shortage of outraged comment from correspondents to the local paper, but little of it was analytical or constructive in the way that Chandler rightly felt was needed. In March 1963 he responded to an article in the Chester Chronicle that had painted a particularly gloomy picture of the state of preservation, stating that on the contrary things were improving. Unlike the time when the Chester Civic Trust was first set up, he maintained, it was no longer necessary for its committee to interest itself in every new planning proposal in the city, so there was more time to spend doing pro-active work. He was shrewdly conscious too of the need to work with rather than against the two Councils, and argued in the case of the Clemences debacle that strong public support was needed if the Corporation was to be able to resist the powerful and persistent pressure from private interests. In a perceptive report written in October 1965 about the formation of the Trust, he reflected on the issues they had had to confront. To find the right balance between preservation and change was the Trust's aim, and this he felt could not be achieved in a system where decisions were made ad hoc, often too late and in a rush. What was urgently needed, he clearly foresaw, was a properly thought-out plan for preservation, and in calling for this, the Trust anticipated the next and crucial stage in Chester's late 20th century development. ■

1965 Public Relations – and the Civic Trust

Dr Quentin Hughes, one of the founder members of Chester Civic Trust and a lecturer in architecture at Liverpool University who co-ordinated the Trust's Bridge Street Improvement Scheme, gave an interesting lecture to a meeting in Manchester in 1965 when he discussed the role of the Civic Trust.

It was at a time when the Chester Civic Trust was pressing for the publication of planning proposals and the opportunity to comment on them before they were considered by councillors.

Quentin Hughes cited fifteenth century Florence where, he said, all major proposals on artistic matters were publicised for general discussion both before and during their construction. He also quoted a Chester City Councillor who had suggested that all major projects for the centre of the city should be put on view. Quentin Hughes pointed out that Chester Civic Trust supported this idea; the public could then be involved in the discussion and their views heard before decisions were taken. To illustrate his point he mentioned three ways in which he thought proposals were handled at that time.

The first was where the promoters throw a large cocktail party and, inviting those they think might be interested, say, *"What to you think about our scheme?"*. They present a model, drawings, and photographs; we make a few comments and say, *"This is wonderful – It's really public-spirited of you to put this show on before you start building"*. They ask for our comments and we give them and they go ahead, take no notice and build the job. Still, Quentin Hughes said, we do have a good cocktail party!

The second group of promoters, according to Quentin Hughes, were those who try to keep quiet until details leak out, then by delays and procrastination try to hush up the comments as far as possible, hoping that once the job is done, there is little that can be done to alter it. People can be as rude as they like about the completed building, but once it is built it stays.

His third group, often operating from distant towns like London or Glasgow, somehow get the message through to their large office that Chester is an historic city. *"Ah" they say, "we must be careful, better play it safe, we'll do an historic design. We don't know much about half-timber construction, so we'll do a Georgian façade. That will be all right"*.

At that time Chester Civic Trust was influential in ensuring that future planning proposals would be publicised and an opportunity given for comment to be made before they were considered, at that time, by the City Council's Improvement Committee. Present members of the Civic Trust may recognise the continuing existence of the third group identified by Quentin Hughes! ■

1965 Chandler's Viewpoint

James Chandler, Chester Civic Trust's first honorary secretary, was acutely aware of the need to inform and influence the general public; his Viewpoint articles in the local press over a period of two years were excellent publicity for the work of the Trust. In fortnightly articles, each with a photograph and accompanying commentary, he illustrated good and bad examples of local development.

Whilst the series was sponsored by the Trust *"with the object of arousing public interest in architectural and similar matters and promoting discussion"*, Chandler observed that his views were not necessarily the opinions of the Trust as a whole or any particular section of its members. Indeed in a forthright letter to Civic Trust Council members he observed that *"public relations were less trouble if the secretary does it himself."* The articles were, however, a serious and informative contribution which, by their publication over a lengthy period, also demonstrated the willingness of the local press to be involved in the planning and architectural concerns of the Trust.

After five years as secretary, Chandler had concluded that the Trust should spend less time organising functions for members and should devote most of its time and money educating the general public. As an example he quoted the

showcase in the Grosvenor Precinct which was first brought into use for the display of the Viewpoint articles. He also thought the Trust had tried to do too much. *"We should do less and do it really thoroughly"* he wrote. And something had to be done about the duration of the Trust's Council meetings which he considered *"should start punctually and go on no longer than an hour and a half, or at the most, two hours."* In his characteristic manner he urged that: *"If this can only be achieved by occasional harsh words from the chair - let them be spoken"*. Good advice for all organisations! ■

FIVE Conservation in action

The Plan for the Central Area prepared by George Grenfell Baines in 1964 had as its underlying objective the economic regeneration of Chester. For Grenfell Baines the key factors were resolving traffic congestion and stimulating development. Whilst he understood the need to protect Chester's unique historic character, he gave no special consideration to the problems of decaying historic fabric. As the national economy expanded and pressure for development grew, more old buildings were falling victim to neglect and demolition. Changes in retailing, where the owner no longer lived over the shop, combined with clearance of the remaining working-class housing in the centre meant that the area within the walls was virtually devoid of residents, and therefore empty at night. Depopulation in turn led to churches becoming redundant and threatened with closure. Whilst the Trust had some notable successes in this period – it persuaded the Council to abandon plans to demolish Georgian houses in Queen Street and to acquire and renovate the Nine Houses in Park Street for example – the development of a strategic approach to conservation came only through a government initiative.

The 'Nine Houses' in Park Street before and after renovation.

The Rt. Hon. Richard Crossman MP.

In 1966, during a brief but stimulating period as Minister for Housing and Local Government for the Labour Government, Richard Crossman selected four historic towns to act as pilot studies to explore how conservation strategies might be framed and implemented. Together with Bath, Chichester and York, Chester was one of the four towns which agreed to commission specialist reports jointly with the government. Donald Insall and Associates was appointed to produce the study on Chester, which was carried out in 1966-67. Insall, whose previous work had included studies of Lavenham in Suffolk and Newark in Nottinghamshire, discovered a city without a clear vision, dependent on its special identity for its economic survival, but with its historic buildings often vulnerable and in a critical state of decay. In a comprehensive analysis he looked at the city in its regional context, at the pressures for change, at traffic and movement, image and identity, and at the specific factors that were impacting on the character of the historic environment. At the detailed level, his team surveyed over 400 historic buildings and developed a series of actions for 10 specific study areas, with three areas for further study. He planned a five-year initial repair programme for 142 buildings; a subsequent ten-year programme for

a further 229; release of City Council land for residential development; acquisition of privately owned land and buildings; and redevelopment by Housing Associations. He also proposed an action plan for listing the city's buildings by a defined date, 1975, revising the listing grades, and the publication of the lists in a more accessible form, changes that found their way into the 1968 Town and Country Planning Act. The report *Chester: A Study in Conservation* provided a practical framework for reconciling the pressure for economic development with the protection of the city's outstanding historic character, and in an article describing the launch, Insall made an urgent plea: 'We hope it will not just be a book on the shelf, but a living and continuing plan for Chester'.

Insall's efforts were not in vain, and to the City Council's credit, his report was accepted in full, with agreement to establish an active Conservation Programme. A Conservation Fund was established with matched funding from central government, and in 1971 England's first Conservation Officer was appointed to manage the programme. Around the same time, Tony Bocking was drawn from the planning team at Norwich to serve as Head of Planning, whilst Donald Insall himself was retained as consultant. In the same year, the Chester Conservation Area Advisory Committee was established with representation from a wide cross section of local organisations and professional associations.

Continued on page 55→

1969-71 The Insall Report: The Trust responds

The immediate reaction of Chester Civic Trust to the long awaited publication of the report was to welcome both its contents and recommendations. Dr John Tomlinson, the Trust's secretary said *"we are glad to find Mr Insall supports some of the recommendations which the Civic Trust has made over the last few years, notably in the use of St Mary's Hill area for residential accommodation"*. It was studied in detail by a special committee consisting of James Chandler, Peter Shobbrook, Gerald Beech, John Makinson and Dr John Tomlinson, with a view to looking at the details of the report and for ways in which the Trust could give support to the City Council in implementing the recommendations of the report.

There was an early proposal to launch a 'Save Chester Fund' to purchase derelict property which would then be repaired and leased. Gerald Beech was deputed to speak to City Council representatives and, had it come to fruition, it could have been the forerunner of the Chester Historic Buildings Preservation Trust, which was to be formed ten years later.

In the months immediately following the publication of the report there were talks between the Trust and the Chester Society of Architects, which had been formed in 1964, concerning a suggestion that money should be raised by public subscription to put into effect some part of the Insall Report. Meetings were also being arranged by the Trust with the Council for the Preservation of Rural England (C P R E) to discuss the report and, in November 1969, Chester Civic Trust convened a meeting of nine

Publication of the report, completed in 1968, was delayed until early 1969 due to a strike at the HMSO warehouse. There were complaints that only a few copies were available in Chester when the report was launched and, at £7 a copy, this was considered to be an excessive price to pay in 1969. The local press – the Chester Chronicle and Cheshire Observer – gave the report extensive and supportive publicity and ensured that Insall's recommendations were widely known in the city.

local societies. Their representatives then met with the Chairmen of the City Council's Improvement and Finance Committees, Vernon Cotterell and Norman Ribbeck, to press for the implementation of a first-aid programme of repairs and the appointment of an officer whose sole responsibility would be to deal with the Insall Report. ∎

1970 The Conservation Fund

The City Council established the Conservation Fund in 1970 as part of the implementation of proposals in the Insall report and in response to the public support for conservation. It was the first local authority to establish such a fund, a special feature of which was that it accrued interest and, unlike most Council budgets, the money did not have to be spent in a particular year. Thus funds could be built-up over a period of years to provide grants (normally 50 per cent towards eligible repair costs) for the most expensive repair schemes.

In the first year a contribution of £29,200 – the equivalent of a 2d rate – was matched by a similar contribution from the government through an arrangement known as a 'Town Scheme'.

By 1980 the annual contribution from the Council had risen to £200,000, also matched by the government. By encouraging owners to repair and improve their own buildings with grants and specialist advice from the City's Conservation Team, it was thought likely that many more buildings would be repaired and the available money used as effectively as possible. Buildings were only acquired by the Council as a last resort to ensure their survival.

Chester Civic Trust has always supported the City Council's approach to funding, especially when inflation and the need for urgent repairs required a substantial increase in the contribution to the Conservation Fund. There were also times when the Trust came to the rescue of the conservation fund.

In 1982, the Trust's chairman Denys Doxat-Pratt, and secretary Denys Goose, wrote to Councillors expressing the deep anxiety felt by the Civic Trust at a proposed cut in the Conservation Fund for the following financial year and expressing concern that any cutback in grants for conservation would have a direct bearing on the economy of the city. They reminded councillors that the *Conservation Review Study*, prepared for the Council in 1976, had identified nearly 300 buildings or groups of buildings requiring repairs; many of the most urgent 'first priority' buildings had not yet been completed and buildings such as Kings Buildings and 1 Abbey Green had still to be started.

At that time the proposal was to cut the contribution to the conservation fund from £210,000 to £90,000 and, with the consequential reduction in matching grants from the government, the total grant availability would be cut from £460,000 to £260,000. When private contributions were taken into account, the conservation work in the city would have been cut by nearly half a million pounds in 1983. Indeed, the Trust urged an increase to catch up with the backlog of necessary work and to keep up with inflation. Surely, they said, this was a small price to pay to ensure that Chester kept its rightful position as one of the most interesting and attractive cities in Europe.

The Trust's timely intervention prompted headlines in the local press, and further representations to the council. When the budget proposals were considered by the City Council, the contribution to the conservation fund was only reduced to £189,000, mitigated by a reduction in the grant under the 'Town Scheme' from 50 to

40 per cent, which did not subsequently appear to affect the implementation of grant-aided repairs. With the addition of accrued interest to the conservation fund it ensured that an amount in excess of £200.000 had been assured for grants in each of the following three years.

This was not an isolated occasion when the Trust found it necessary to ask councillors to rethink their proposals. By 1992 the City Council's annual contributions to the conservation fund had been reduced to £68,000 and it was proposed to further reduce the amount to £50,000 for the following financial year.

Referring to the Civic Trust's concerns, the Chester Chronicle reported that *"a watchdog group fears Chester's heritage could suffer after revelations that the city council aims to slash its conservation grants"*. And in a letter to all the council's party leaders, the Trust emphasised that *"the conservation rate has previously received all-party support as essential to the success and continuity of the city's conservation programme."*

In retrospect, it has been acknowledged that the Trust was a major influence in ensuring the cross-party support in the City Council for conservation funding which was the envy of many local authorities. ∎

The decision represented a huge shift in attitude: where the City Council had previously resisted spending money on repairs to historic buildings such as the Blue Bell, now it was prepared to levy a specific 'conservation rate'. From a tendency to accept the demolition of historic buildings, it agreed to use its legal powers proactively to enforce repair and compulsory purchase. Insall's recommendations for greater traffic constraints were endorsed, and a plan of maintenance and enhancement of the public realm was adopted. As the programme developed over subsequent years, it was seen as a beacon of good conservation practice and the City Council was duly rewarded with three separate national and international awards.

Support and endorsement by government was also crucial to the successful adoption of the programme, and of Insall's strategic recommendations – the only one that failed to gain acceptance was for a

national corporation for historic towns on a par with the New Towns Commission.

One of the first actions, in January 1969, was to designate the whole of the commercial centre of the city – an area of 80 hectares – as a conservation area, and in December of that year the ambitious Conservation Programme was approved. In the early years effort was concentrated on three major issues: the restoration of key historic buildings; coordinated action in the Bridgegate area; and controlling new development to encourage sympathetic design. The idea of focusing on Bridgegate was to demonstrate how an area could be rescued through heritage-based regeneration. A temporary office was established in the area as a point of liaison with local people, and detailed inspections were carried out of 77 buildings. 49 of these were found to be in need of substantial repair and improvement, of which a number were acquired by the Council for renovation and subsequent resale. This was supported

Derelict housing in Shipgate Street.

Shipgate House: a major restoration completed in 1971 by the County Council.

by funding from the Department of the Environment. The critical state of the buildings was alarmingly highlighted when the roof of the consultants' Bridgegate office suddenly collapsed. The first buildings to be tackled were those on the west side of Lower Bridge Street, including Shipgate House by the County Council and Gamul House by the City Council, together with the terraced houses in Gamul Place. Sympathetically designed high density housing units were fitted into gap sites and backland areas. The Falcon Inn, one of the most important timber-framed buildings in the city, was rescued by a specially formed charitable trust and re-established as a public house, whilst public uses were found for three of the redundant churches in the area, St Michael, St Mary on the Hill and St Olave.

Gamul Place before and after.

Gamul House before and after.

Lower Bridge Street before and after.

Reviewing progress in 1973, two years after his appointment as the first Conservation Officer, Roger Tilley explained the complexities of managing the programme. Patterns of ownership in Chester are unusually complicated, with different floors of Row properties commonly being in separate ownership. As a result, the City Council took the initiative, appointing local architectural practices to carry out structural surveys and make detailed recommendations. These surveys formed the basis for repair schedules on which the cost estimates were based.

Roger Tilley.

 ## 1971 The Conservation Area Advisory Committee

Nine local societies were convened by Chester Civic Trust to discuss the Insall Report. After their representatives had met City Council chairmen, the Trust's Vice President, James Chandler, emphasised the extremely friendly way in which they had been received at the Town Hall. It had been agreed that a Conservation Area Advisory Committee should be set up consisting of one member from each of the nine organisations. The Trust decided that James Chandler should represent them and that the Trust's viewpoint on any matter should be decided by James Chandler and Gerald Beech, together with Gerald Burkinshaw, Chester's Town Clerk until his retirement in 1969 when he immediately became a valued member (and later Chairman) of Chester Civic Trust.

In 1971 Chester became the first city to form a Conservation Area Advisory Committee (CAAC) and, later that year, the Department of the Environment advised all historic cities and towns to set up similar bodies which could be consulted on developments planned in their conservation areas.

When the advisory committee was being formed a Chester architect, Gilbert Parry, was President of the Chester (later Cheshire) Society of Architects and represented that society at the formative meetings. He became the first chairman of the advisory committee, serving in that position for many years. More recently, several Civic Trust members have given devoted service to the committee, among them John Wakeman, Oliver Bott, Peter Boughton and John Herson.

In the forty years since its formation, there have been a few changes in the composition of CAAC although Chester Civic Trust has remained a member throughout this period. There are still nine societies and organisations which are each entitled to send a representative and, additionally, there is one independent member. The committee continues to meet regularly to examine and comment on planning applications within the conservation areas and to receive presentations from architects on major development proposals. ■

Castle Street before and after.

Much of the spend was to go into repairing roofs and guttering, which made no dramatic impact on the appearance of the buildings, but ensured that rapid decay was halted. The Conservation Officer's job was also made more difficult by the acute shortage of technical skills and expertise in the local construction industry which sometimes meant that work had to be redone.

In 1974, local government reorganisation led to the amalgamation of Chester City, Chester Rural District and Tarvin Rural District Councils to form the new Chester District Council. A key appointment was that of Cyril Morris, who moved from being Assistant County Architect to become Director of Technical Services for the new authority. At the County, Morris had been responsible for the Police HQ, the library building programme and the County's conservation projects. Following his appointment, the city's conservation team was strengthened, whilst a more professional and better coordinated approach to the new authority's architectural, engineering and planning functions was fostered, not only in the city centre, but also throughout the rural towns and villages. Morris was personally

attracted to the new post by the prospect of managing the implementation of Donald Insall's proposals, and in this task he was keenly supported by Tony Bocking through planning policies and development control, and by successive chairmen of the Development and Planning Committee.

With the completion of the ring road in 1972, measures were gradually introduced to reduce traffic in the central streets. Whilst this was opposed at virtually every stage by a majority of retailers, the closure of the Cross, and later of parts of Eastgate Street and Northgate Street brought immediate improvements and a significant rise in shopping activity, contrary to the expectations of the retailers. Thus traffic management and incremental pedestrianisation ran in tandem with the conservation initiatives, and raised the quality of life in the city centre.

European Architectural Heritage Year, 1975, acted as a focus for conservation in Chester. The Bridgegate Action Area was selected by the government as one of two major pilot projects in England, giving much national and international attention to Chester's conservation

In 1973 the Chairman of the UK Committee for European Architectural Heritage Year, the Countess of Dartmouth (later Countess Spencer), visited Chester to discuss the City's preparations for 1975. The photograph shows her inspecting a model of the Bridgegate Action Area with (from left to right) Vernon Cotterell (Chairman of the City's Improvement Committee), Cyril Morris (Assistant County Architect), Hugh Jones, (Chairman of the Shadow Development and Planning Committee), Jack Whittle (County Architect) and Donald Insall (Conservation Consultant).

methods. The Chester Civic Trust organised a series of activities throughout the year, and arranged for the High Cross to be reinstated in its original location in front of St Peter's Church which became a traffic free area. The year began with a BBC TV programme on New Year's Day, in which the Duke of Edinburgh gave his views on conservation. Urging the public to 'knock on doors and write to the local papers', he suggested that people should look around and criticise local government planners, architects and experts, something that the citizens of Chester hardly needed to be encouraged to do. In the city a highlight of the year was the opening of the Heritage Centre in St Michael's Church. Around that time Donald Insall set out his own philosophy on the old debate between keeping a historic town alive and freezing it as a museum piece:

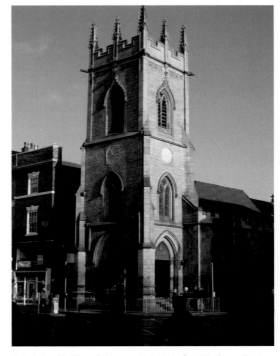

St Michael's Church became Britain's first Heritage Centre.

The Duke & Duchess of Gloucester officially opening the Chester Heritage Centre in June 1975. They are seen here with (left) Cyril Morris, Director of Technical Services and (right) Councillor Hugh Jones, Chairman of the Development & Planning Committee.

'Conservation in Britain is an integral part of land-use planning...a guiding influence upon the process of change... The art-historian philosophy is most dangerous – you cannot 'put-back' a town to its original state – what is the 'original' in a living town? What one can do is to incorporate sympathetically into it, and then enjoy those earlier human strata that are so precious to it'.

In 1982 Donald Insall's progress report on the Bridgegate area was published by the government entitled *Conservation in Action*. It offered 10 lessons which could be applied to the problems found in historic towns across the country and indeed across the world. These ranged from the need to understand the bigger picture, in which the conservation programme was linked firmly to economic and social objectives, to the assembly of a well-coordinated and properly resourced conservation team. Within a firm strategy,

a flexible and common sense approach to regulations was recommended. Building confidence, developing good communications and engendering goodwill were found to be vital tools to effective action, and where the local authority was prepared to set an example, the chances of private owners following suit was considered more likely. As a result of the emerging success of the Bridgegate project, two further action areas were agreed: the Cathedral Precinct and Queen Street/Canalside, though following local government reorganisation in 1974, cuts in the City Council's budget were to constrain progress on these initiatives for two or three years, which was only partly offset by an increase in government funding.

There was also significant progress in the management of archaeology in the city since the losses that had been sustained in the development frenzy of the 1960s. In

One of the many visitors to the new Heritage Centre was Environment Minister Baroness Birk, seen here with Donald Insall and Tony Bocking (Chief Planning Officer).

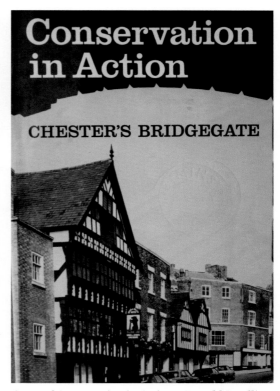

Cover of Conservation in Action – Donald Insall's progress report on the Bridgegate Action Area.

1972 a properly-resourced Archaeological Unit had been set up at the Grosvenor Museum, and in 1979 Chester was made a national Area of Archaeological Importance, which gave the Unit the ability to investigate and record archaeology ahead of any redevelopment schemes. This led to significant finds being made for example at Abbey Green, and on the bus exchange and library site off the Town Hall Square.

During the mid 1970s, a number of writers for architectural and planning journals visited the city to see how the conservation programme was operating. Anne Dennier, writing in *The Town Planning Review* of 1975, observed that the degree of accord in Chester differed from both Bath and York, where conservation policies and planning decisions had aroused heated controversy. In Chester she found the Chester Civic Trust and

the Council for the Preservation of Rural England (CPRE) working in co-operation with the Council. Tony Aldous wrote a sympathetic account in 1977, citing the greatest achievement as the introduction of traffic controls, which had allowed the city centre to resume its traditional function as the natural meeting place for citizens and visitors, the hub where people could once again stroll, walk and talk in comfort and pleasure. John Cornforth, who wrote two well-researched pieces for *Country Life* felt that the method developed in Chester should act as a model for other historic cities, and stressed the importance of conservation management and learning appropriate management skills.

With all this positive feedback during the early years of the conservation programme, it came as a shock when

The Falcon before and after.

Michael Heseltine visited Chester in 1980 to see progress on the City's conservation programme. He is seen here inspecting the Falcon with (from left) Cyril Morris (Director of Technical Services), Donald Insall (Conservation Consultant), the Mayor of Chester (Councillor Hugh Jones) and Peter Pritchard (Contractor).

The Falcon plaque.

the *Architects Journal* published a fiercely critical article on Chester by Gillian Darley in May 1978. She observed that 10 years on from the historic towns report, a walk around the walls revealed not so much the 'tourist's view of Victorio-medieval facades' but more the abused fabric of the city despite its conservation-conscious image and special status. Notwithstanding the money and expertise that had been available, Chester, she maintained, represented a fallacy in conservation policy where the research, planning and resources expended on historic fabric had not been integrated with the wider fabric of the city. The city centre, isolated within its walls and inner ring road, had become a ghetto of shops and offices, sprinkled with waste spaces and derelict buildings. The fault, as she saw it, arose from Insall's brief, which had concentrated on the city core, and revealed a misunderstanding on the part of the Ministry of Housing and Local Government of how cities work. The impetus of European Architectural Heritage Year 1975, which had concentrated effort on fewer, larger projects, rather than spreading it more widely had only reinforced this schism.

She also regretted that more muscle had not been brought to bear on the two major landowners in the city – the Dean and Chapter of the Cathedral, and the Grosvenor Estate, noting that three of the 16 buildings most at risk in the 1976 review were cathedral properties, whilst the Grosvenor Estate had let the Falcon Inn in Lower Bridge Street fall into ruinous condition. In the case of the Falcon, she reported that although negotiations had eventually led to the building being transferred to a Trust and repaired, it took 10 years to do so. Two other major owners were also an embarrassment, the City and County Councils. Each owned blocks of Georgian housing in Shipgate Street standing empty and decaying, and she questioned the heavy restoration of the Dutch House in Bridge Street and the Bear and Billet where much of the original structure had been replaced.

Dutch Houses, Bridge Street.

Bear & Billet, Lower Bridge Street.

Turning to the new architecture of Chester, she found no cause for optimism, regarding a display that had been put on at the Heritage Centre as 'depressing'. The Forum she described as dismal, and she was dismissive also of the two most recent office developments – Windsor House on the corner of Pepper Street and Lower Bridge Street, designed by Edmund Kirby & Son, and Centurion House, Northgate Street, home of HM Customs, by Robin Clayton. She was alarmed by the rate of commercial and retail permissions being granted, which were far in excess of consultants' recommended limits, and noted that Arrowcroft's scheme north of

Windsor House on the corner of Pepper Street and Lower Bridge Street.

Arrowcroft Shopping Scheme - View from Foregate Street.

Centurion House, Northgate Street.

The Queen Street chapel prior to relocation.

Foregate Street designed by Benoy and Partners would lead to the destruction of several listed buildings including the distinguished Queen Street Chapel and Sunday School, replacing them with meaningless reconstructed facades. Within the Walls, consent had been granted for shopping and car parking on Commonhall Street, and more had been approved on Lower Bridge Street. 'The loss of all urban functions save tourism, shopping and office employment seems an odd manifestation of a conservation policy', she scathingly remarked. Whilst not denying the good work that was being done within the conservation programme, her final thrust was a warning of the dangers of a massive over-provision of shopping, with its attendant problems, and the headaches that it would surely bring in the future. This was a view that would be expressed repeatedly, and equally firmly dismissed, over the following 30 years. ∎

1975 European Architectural Heritage Year

In June 1973 the Bridgegate Action Area was selected as one of the four pilot projects to represent the United Kingdom for European Architectural Heritage Year in 1975. The others were in Edinburgh, Poole and the County of Fife.

Chester Heritage City Logo.

Selection of the Bridgegate Area gave an impetus to conservation work throughout the city and Chester's approach to the problems of urban conservation attracted national and international attention. Chester Civic Trust members joined in the special events of the year including study tours, exhibitions and a lecture by Dr Patrick Nuttgens arranged by the Trust in association with the Cheshire Society of Architects and the Society of 13.

The Trust's permanent contribution to European Architectural Heritage Year was the reinstatement of the city's medieval High Cross, taken from the Roman crossroads during Cromwell's siege of Chester, to its rightful place in front of St Peter's Church.

This symbolic 'improvement' was made possible by the decision of the City Council to 'Cut The Cross', barring the staggered junction at the heart of Chester to all vehicles. The Cross became once more the hub of things- for people, not vehicles. As Donald Insall said at the time *"That gives me greater pleasure than almost anything else"*. Life had returned to the centre of Chester. ■

The Rows were featured on one of the Royal Mail stamps for European Architectural Heritage Year.

The Cross - Work in progress.

The High Cross is restored to its original location in front of St Peter's Church.

1975 The Bell Tower, Chester Cathedral

In the late 1960's Chester Civic Trust was asked for its views on the proposed Bell Tower by the Royal Fine Art Commission and replied:-

"If the need for a bell tower is accepted at all, then it should be achieved in as modern a style, representative of the 20th century, as possible."

Designed by George Pace and named the Addleshaw Tower after the Dean of Chester, it was officially opened by HRH The Duke of Gloucester in June 1975 during his visit to celebrate European Architectural Heritage Year. It was the first detached bell tower to be built for a cathedral in this country since the Reformation and was listed Grade II in 2012.■

The Bell Tower.

SIX Chester at the crossroads

Contrary to Gillian Darley's fears, the city centric emphasis of the Conservation Programme turned out to be one of its greatest strengths, for it helped to build confidence and encourage private sector investment in the formerly run down action areas. Indeed by the time Darley visited the city, a host of smaller projects were underway at the same time as the major conservation schemes in order to build momentum. In due course the programme was widened to include sites outside the walls, whilst additional action areas took in the riverside, Egerton Street and The Bars. But the problems in the centre were generally more complex and deep-rooted. For example, the underuse and vacancy of upper floors in historic buildings was a major cause of neglect and decay. A pilot study carried out in 1979 in the Rows showed that disuse was related not only to upper floors, but also to the rear of properties. This suggested the need to

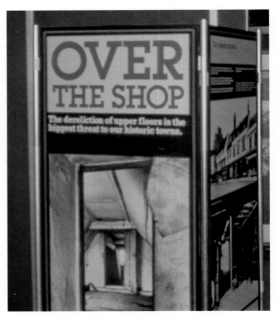

Decaying upper floors 'Over the Shop' exhibition screen 1982.

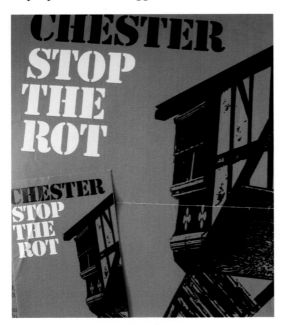

Stop the Rot poster and brochure.

deal holistically with groups of buildings to find solutions, based on an understanding of uses, ownership and tenancies, and on access and circulation. In the past these areas had often been penetrated by a network of small alleys and courtyards, giving independent access to upper floors and backs of properties which, if opened up, could reactivate landlocked spaces. As a result of the study, an exhibition and film was shown in the Heritage Centre entitled *Chester – Stop the Rot*, which contributed to the national debate about the underuse of upper floors.

Darley was rightly critical of the general quality of the new architecture erected in the city in the 1960s and 70s. On the one hand the Pepper Street façade of the Grosvenor Precinct and the crude outline of Commerce House in Hunter Street are examples of a total disregard for context.

The C & A Store (now Primark) in Foregate Street.

Muir Housing Canalside.

On the other, Heritage Court in Lower Bridge Street shows a paper-thin and weak attempt at replicating traditional forms. But there were good examples of contemporary buildings designed in a studied version of the local style, the best being the former C&A store, now Primark, in Foregate Street erected in 1970 and designed by Building Design Partnership. This reflects the Chester vernacular in the use of a colonnade with the building projecting over the street, the bold modelling of the façade with repeated bay features, and through the use of vestigial infill panels in the top storey. Its freshness and imaginative qualities have stood the test of time. But more modest schemes have also made a lasting contribution. The sensitive canalside housing for the Muir Group Housing Association by Design Group Partnership, and the cleverly planned housing off Castle Street by the same architects in conjunction with Insalls are inconspicuous by the way they naturally fit into the grain of the areas. Perhaps the best housing scheme of this period is the Shipgate development designed by James C Sanders, based on a concept by Donald Insall Associates, in the form of a tightly-grouped complex of flats and maisonettes set above a semi-basement car park, with a cascade of glazed conservatories overlooking the river.

Continued on page 74→

Shipgate - New housing.

1968 Lectures and currant buns

Chester Civic Trust prides itself on the quality and content of its lectures and publications.

Lectures have always been well supported but perhaps none more so than that given by Dr John Tomlinson, secretary of the Trust from 1967 to 1969, entitled *Chester 1868 – 1968 in Photographs*. In a personal reminiscence in 2000 he recalled his lecture in 1968 to advertise both the Chester Photographic Survey and the Civic Trust. Expecting about 30 people he hired a small room in the Grosvenor Hotel but when those arriving reached 200 the manager of the hotel decided to move everyone into the ballroom. At least 300 people attended and John Tomlinson commented that *"I was astonished and didn't think people would be so interested"*. A book of photographs followed which sold ten thousand copies followed by a reprint which sold another five thousand!

John Tomlinson also remembered places in Chester which were familiar to him including Clemences, Quaintways and Densons, and which have since gone. He recalled his schooldays with an amusing reminiscence:

"When I was at the Choir School in the War, we were allowed out for a break in the morning to go round the Market Square. We would all go to Clemences to get a bun – you could get a penny bun, an ordinary round one with currants in it. You could get a longer one for tuppence, and we were always besieged by King's School boys at the gate, who weren't allowed out, to go and buy buns for them. We ought to have charged commission!

Chester's Popular Restaurant
Nearest to CATHEDRAL and TOWN HALL.

Clemences

LUNCHEONS, TEAS
DINNERS, SUPPERS

Finest Cooking.   Excellent Service.   SPECIAL
TERMS for Choir Parties, etc.   CATERING
of Every Description for Town and Country.
Bakers.   Confectioners.   Pastrycooks.
Bride Cake Specialists. ∘ *Chocolates.*

ADDRESSES :
TOWN HALL SQUARE, CHESTER
and HIGH STREET, MOLD.
'Phone: CHESTER 54.   'Phone : MOLD 44.

Clemences was marvellous for dances. School dances were held there and then Quaintways took over as you got older. Then there were the League of Pity Balls. The League of Pity was the junior branch of the NSPCC and started a fundraising ball for teenagers. They were so popular that mothers would offer bribes to get their daughters a ticket in the hope of meeting a nice boy. They had three hundred places and there was always a waiting list. That was in the old ballroom at the Grosvenor before it was modernised. It was an old county town hotel, almost like Jane Austen's days, before they glossed it up in the 1960s when they developed the Precinct." ∎

1968 Leo, the brewery lion

Today, the lion stands on top of the car park adjacent to the Newgate.

When the former Bent's Lion Brewery was being demolished in 1968, James Chandler wondered whether the lion could be saved. He spoke to Dr John Tomlinson, the Trust's Secretary, and asked, *"What are we going to do with the lion? How do we get it down? Where do we keep it?"* John Tomlinson decided that he would be responsible. An Army officer he knew offered to arrange transport and the next thing he heard was that a low-loader had arrived on site. It had happened so quickly that he hadn't decided where it could be stored. He recalls that he

Leo re-sited.

left his patients in the surgery and the lion was taken to his home in Curzon Park.

By 1971 Dr Tomlinson had moved to Hampshire, leaving Leo in his garden. The new multi-storey car park, designed by the Biggins Sargent Partnership was nearing completion on the site of the former brewery. James Latham suggested that the lion should be placed in its present position, on top of the prominent concrete staircase tower of the car park. The suggestion was favourably received and the architects arranged to move the lion from Curzon Park to its new home in October 1971.

Thanks to the Doctor, Leo had been saved from certain death! ■

Leo being rescued.

The most hotly debated building was the County Police HQ, which has always divided opinion. Grenfell Baines had been closely involved in the development of the scheme with the County Architect, Edgar Taberner and his staff, and Donald Insall regarded it as an example of beneficial change. In 1969, two years after its completion, it received a national Civic Trust Award for 'its contribution to the appearance of the local scene', whilst the textured concrete end wall by the sculptor William Mitchell was chosen as one of ten examples in Britain for inclusion in a UNESCO publication designed to show international examples of the effective use of art in modern architecture. Nikolaus Pevsner, on the other hand, called it 'extremely objectionably sited', disliking the way it presented 'a windowless wall with an aggressive all-over concrete relief' towards the propylaea of the castle. Yet the building, which survived for scarcely 40 years, was an intelligent and carefully

Police Headquarters from Chester Castle.

considered architectural statement, arguably the finest work of 20th century architecture in the city, set in a sympathetic landscape designed by Derek

Police Headquarters from Nuns Road.

Lovejoy and Partners. Unfortunately both building and landscape suffered serious abuse at the hands of the Constabulary, which added an ugly array of radio antennae to the roof, neglected the reflecting pool flanking the entrance approach, and erected large metal barriers around the perimeter greensward to keep people away. Loved neither by its occupants nor the wider public, when the police moved out to Winsford in 2003, the by now tarnished Headquarters building was doomed.

In the '60s and '70s not only did the Chester Civic Trust take a keen interest in Chester's future planning, but the Chester and District Junior Chamber of Commerce also produced a number of well-informed reports to encourage better management of the historic environment. These included *Tomorrow's Tourist*, which was the first comprehensive study of the tourism industry in Chester, and *The Groves: Development or Decay?*, an action plan for the improvement of the riverfront. In May 1969, at much the same time that Insall's report was published, the Junior Chamber brought out *Chester at the Crossroads?*, a radical proposal for traffic management in the city centre that was intended to counter the perception on the part of traders that pedestrianisation would adversely affect their business. With the aim of maintaining the city's status as a regional tourism and retail centre with an attractive environment, they advocated an experimental pedestrianisation scheme, leading to a permanent segregation of vehicles and pedestrians in all the central streets. This was to be accompanied by comprehensive environmental improvements.

A response to *Chester at the Crossroads?* was included in the City Council's traffic plan that emerged in 1970. The

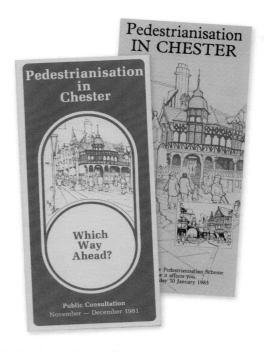

Pedestrianisation leaflets.

plan was written by A D Statham, the City Engineer and Surveyor, who recommended a very cautious approach. Reviewing the various plans that had been produced for the city centre, he dismissed Grenfell Baines's suggestions for bus lanes, noting that nothing of that sort had been implemented anywhere in the UK at the time. As to pedestrianising Bridge Street and Watergate Street, also proposed by Grenfell Baines, he did not see how this could be done without first creating rear service areas. Insalls' modest traffic proposals were considered to be premature, whilst the plan produced by the Junior Chamber to close Bridge Street, Watergate Street, Eastgate Street, St Werburgh Street and part of Northgate Street between 10.30am and 7.00pm and reroute all the buses to service the extremities of the pedestrian areas was dismissed as not being in the interests of the city.

Continued on page 78→

1979 Grosvenor Bridge model

In 1968 Chester Civic Trust carried out repairs to the original sandstone model of Thomas Harrison's Grosvenor Bridge, then on display in the Water Tower Gardens. Eight years later a member of the Trust drew attention to the condition of the model and suggested that it should be located nearer to the Grosvenor Bridge and in a position more visible to the public.

Various sites were suggested, the most favoured being on the western side of the castle moat, near to Castle Drive and the Little Roodee. H A Clegg & Sons, the Chester stonemasons, were willing to move the model to its new site and the Trust decided that work should be completed in time for the 150th anniversary of Thomas Harrison's death in 1829.

The work was duly completed on time, the model being repaired and relocated at the expense of the Trust, with a contribution from Chester Soroptomists towards the cost of the plaque.

When the new site for the model was first suggested, Chester Civic Trust proposed that consideration should be given to floodlighting the Grosvenor Bridge. Floodlighting the City's bridges and historic buildings has been an aspiration of the Trust since that time. It was a happy coincidence that Cheshire County Council, as their contribution to the City's 1900th anniversary - also in 1979 – installed floodlighting to the three bridges over the River Dee, the Suspension Bridge, Old Dee Bridge and Grosvenor Bridge. A slate plaque on the Grosvenor Bridge, carved by the Welsh sculptor Jonah Jones, commemorates the event. Regrettably none of these floodlighting schemes has been maintained. ■

(Opposite) The floodlighting of the Grosvenor Bridge (top) and Old Dee Bridge (bottom) by the County Council, commemorating the City's 1900th anniversary, coincided with the relocation of the model of the Grosvenor Bridge by Chester Civic Trust.

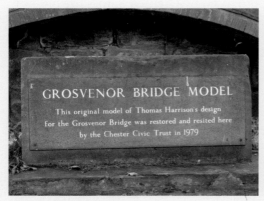

Commemorative plaque.

Model of Grosvenor Bridge.

Traffic congestion at The Cross before pedestrianisation.

Yet pedestrianisation was not totally ruled out; Statham thought it could be desirable to close certain streets in the centre at least at peak times. It was just that he could not accept it as a fundamental part of the plan. The key as he saw it was to get the traffic flowing better, and the first phase was to close The Cross and introduce a loop system from the Inner Ring so that servicing could be continued while ensuring that through traffic was discouraged. The second phase involved closing the ends of various minor streets to stop vehicle runs across the centre, whilst phase three was aimed at encouraging segregation of pedestrians and vehicles, largely by engineering devices such as a subway beneath Grosvenor Road, installing barriers along the road edges and increasing the radius of junctions. As to Bridge Street and Watergate Street, whilst pedestrianisation was not advocated, the plan made allowance for it to be carried out 'as and when it is felt desirable'. It was a timid

proposal, but represented the first small step towards civilising the city centre.

Under Cyril Morris's direction, the new District Council, in conjunction with the County Council as highway authority, adopted a more integrated approach to planning and highways, and in the spring of 1978, a bolder scheme was put forward for public comment. It involved prohibiting vehicles from the main shopping area between 10.30am and 4.30pm and re-routing the buses. But such was the level of opposition from traders and business organisations, that the prohibitions were abandoned, to be replaced by a proposal to remove traffic only on Saturdays. By 1982, however, when the first phase of a combined pedestrianisation and street improvement scheme was introduced, agreement had been reached on closing the streets to traffic from 10.30am to 4.30pm except for loading and unloading of goods, as well as total closure on Saturdays.

Town Hall Square before and after pedestrianisation.

The western part of Eastgate Street was resurfaced in buff concrete blocks. The public response to the scheme was so overwhelmingly positive, that the traders duly agreed to close the streets to all vehicles during the restricted hours. In 1985, Northgate Street was resurfaced using the original granite setts, which were lifted and relaid together with stone paving. Whereas the carpet of concrete blocks in Eastgate Street soon looked tawdry and out of place, the treatment of Northgate Street has remained sound and timeless.

Gillian Darley's most savage criticism had been reserved for what she saw as the massive over-provision of retailing, leading to an imbalance in the mix of city centre uses, which she predicted would create problems in the future. The Chester Civic Trust too observed the increase in retail and commercial floorspace with growing anxiety. Their 1977 Annual Report included an article on the Queen Street – Canalside Redevelopment scheme, which incorporated a superstore, a multi-storey car park and a shopping precinct. Whilst the site had suffered planning blight for so long that most of the buildings had become derelict, making wholesale demolition and redevelopment almost inevitable, they regretted that what was essentially a domestic neighbourhood with an intimate street pattern would be wholly lost. *'As it is'*, they ruefully remarked, *'the commercial gain will mean Chester will become that little less individual and just a little more like everywhere else'*. The statement echoed Grenfell Baines's concerns about the homogeneity of retailing in Chester in 1964, and was to be repeated many times in subsequent years.■

 ### Heritage Walks

In 1979 and 1985 Chester Civic Trust produced two of the four Heritage Walks for Chester City Council. Each walk covered a section of the city and was illustrated with line drawings by different artists. Starting and finishing at the Heritage Centre they enabled a visitor to the city to explore the whole of the area within the City Walls.■

1981 Chester Historic Buildings Preservation Trust (CHBPT)

One of the major initiatives of Chester Civic Trust in the early 1980s was the formation of a buildings preservation trust. At a meeting of members of the Trust and city council officers in late 1979 the city's conservation officer agreed to prepare a list of buildings which might be suitable for a preservation trust to acquire and restore. A steering group was set up with representatives of other amenity societies and in the following twelve months, with financial assistance from Chester Civic Trust, steps were taken to register the new body as a limited company with charitable status.

When the Chester Historic Buildings Preservation Trust (CHBPT) was incorporated as a company on 31st March 1981 it was unusual in that no specific project had been identified. This proved to be an advantage as the newly formed management committee was able to examine several potential buildings, the scale of work required, the purchase price,

loan requirements and the likely re-sale value before they plunged into a complex restoration scheme.

In order to qualify for grants, and take advantage of low–interest loans from the Architectural Heritage Fund, a building or structure had to be special and its restoration commercially uneconomic. Not surprisingly, building preservation trusts are often described as 'the agents of last resort'! Indeed, the very existence of CHBPT proved to be a stimulus to existing owners to restore their buildings in Egerton Street, Bunce Street, Lower Bridge Street and Castle Street with the aid of government and local authority grants.

By 1983, CHBPT was considering the plight of the most neglected buildings in the rural area. Church House in Tarvin, listed Grade II* and the oldest surviving timber-framed building in the village was empty, derelict and in danger of collapse. It was purchased by Chester City Council, and in 1985, passed to CHBPT for restoration. Dr Geoffrey Martin, the first Chairman of CHBPT, was succeeded in 1988 by Dr Allan Pullin, a past chairman of Chester Civic Trust. Under his leadership, an architect (James Brotherhood Associates) was appointed, funding secured and the restoration completed. Church House received a commendation in the 1991 Civic Awards and

Civic Trust members visiting Church House Tarvin before restoration work begins.

Ince Manor before restoration.

Ince Manor near Elton, an empty and derelict Grade I listed building, which was also a scheduled ancient monument, emerged as the Trust's next project. The importance of the surviving Great Hall and Monastery Cottages was evident from the Domesday Book of 1086, which recorded that *"the church itself held and holds Ince"*. It was the home of a monastic community attached to St Werburgh's Abbey in Chester from the 13th century and it is also recorded that Edward I was entertained there by the monks for two nights in 1277. It remained in Church ownership until the death of Henry VIII in 1547.

in the same year was sold as a fine private dwelling.

Well before the sale of Church House, members of the CHBPT were looking for their next project. The so-called Civil War 'field hospital' at Rowton (which, twenty years later, continues to deteriorate) was considered, as were several cottages, redundant chapels, farm buildings and even a windmill!

The first feasibility studies were carried out in 1995 by Donald Insall Associates but the acquisition process was extremely tortuous and lengthy. Denys Doxat-Pratt, also a founder member of CHBPT, became Chairman in 2000 and, after funding had been secured from English Heritage and the Heritage Lottery Fund, supported by a loan

Members of the Council of Management with representatives of the Architectural Heritage Fund and the Association of Preservation Trusts at Ince Manor in 2000.

'Stone laying' at Ince Manor - The Bishop of Chester (The Rt. Revd. Dr. Peter Forster) and Tony Barton (Donald Insall Associates) in 2002.

Ince Manor: inside the re-roofed Hall.

from the Architectural Heritage Fund, work started in 2002. Following the successful completion of the contract, the buildings were sold to an enthusiastic local owner who has continued the work of adaptation and who opens the buildings for the public to view on Heritage Open Days.

The original initiative of Chester Civic Trust in 1981 has been rewarded by the dedicated work of the members of CHBPT, the majority of whom have, throughout the last thirty years, been prominent members of the Trust. However, it must be acknowledged that CHBPT's achievements have been limited to the two projects. Although several others have been investigated, the success of the local authority's conservation programme, combined with the inability of the CHBPT to build up a 'revolving fund', have made it difficult to identify any further viable projects. ■

Ince Manor: View of the restored shell of Monastery Cottages.

SEVEN Glittering prizes

In 1979 Chester commemorated its 1,900th anniversary, an event which provided an opportunity for reassessment of the conservation programme. Summing up at the end of the year, an editorial in the Chester Chronicle suggested that some of the momentum of European Architectural Heritage Year had been lost. Whilst this was no doubt a case of the newspaper manufacturing a story to sell copies (the year had actually been a very active one for conservation in Chester with substantial repairs to the City Walls and the Row steps; the designation of 16 new conservation areas; the service of seven legal notices on historic building owners; the award of 55 grants; and the

initiation of three enhancement schemes), a drop in City Council funding for conservation over the past four years had made it impossible to pursue a number of important schemes. As a result of the demand, it was agreed to more than double the city's annual contribution to £201,000 for 1980/81, which brought in increased funds from the newly formed Department of the Environment towards the city centre 'Town Scheme' and the ability to begin improving some of the historic spaces between buildings. The re-activated programme was rewarded with the 1981 European Prize for the Preservation of Historic Monuments, an honour that was compounded in 1983 when the City Council's work in the

Presentation of the 1981 European Prize for the Preservation of Historic Monuments, left to right: Councillor Heber Fearnall (Chairman of the Development and Planning Committee), Cyril Morris (Director of Technical Services) and Donald Insall (Conservation Consultant).

Bridgegate Area was recognised with a Europa Nostra Award. These awards, and the ambassadorial activities of Insall and Morris, placed Chester squarely on the international stage. Indeed, the mid 1980s was probably the most successful period for conservation in Chester. In 1984 the Duke of Gloucester opened the recently completed scheme for Kings Buildings with the words:

Chester received the prestigious Europa Nostra Award in 1983 for the Bridgegate Conservation Action Area and again in 1989 (jointly with the County Council) for the conservation and enhancement of the City's historical and architectural heritage.

> *'The problem of making a city work is never a simple one. Many Councils send for the bulldozer, but they pay the price in that they are less loved, less popular and more vandalised … Chester is a wonderful example to others. It is a shame when people have to say 'Why didn't we do it like Chester?'*

Gillian Darley had worried that the conservation programme was concentrated too much on the city centre, but over time, the Action Area approach was shown to have achieved success. Most of the principal areas had been defined in the 1968 Insall report, and gradually new ones were added, first on the perimeter of the city and then, following local government re-organisation, in the rural hinterland. In areas such as Bridgegate, confidence had been low and the City Council had to take

In 1985 the Conservation Team received the Royal Town Planning Institute's Silver Jubilee Commendation for Planning Achievement. Pictured, left to right: Andrew Brown (Conservation Officer), Anna McPherson (English Heritage), Donald Insall (Conservation Consultant), Cyril Morris (Director of Technical Services), Lord Elton (Minister of State for the Environment), John Collins (County Planning Officer and past president RTPI), Carol Thickins and Peter Locke (Donald Insall Associates) and (behind) the President of the RTPI, Stephen Byrne.

King's Buildings before and after restoration.

a highly pro-active approach, showing by example what could be achieved. Others such as the Cathedral Precinct or Riverside just required grant support to bridge the deficit between the cost of repairs and the value of the properties on completion.

The most challenging area was the Rows, an outstandingly important, complex and rich heritage resource, subject to continuous and often incompatible commercial pressures. The Insall report identified 12 Row buildings with serious defects, 57 that were deteriorating and only 20 in a satisfactory condition. Poor maintenance over a long period, particularly of shared valley gutters between buildings had hastened decay, as well as disuse of upper floors and problems of access. The Rows are unique in the way that public walkways pass through private properties, and successive city authorities have been responsible for the management of the walkways, stalls,

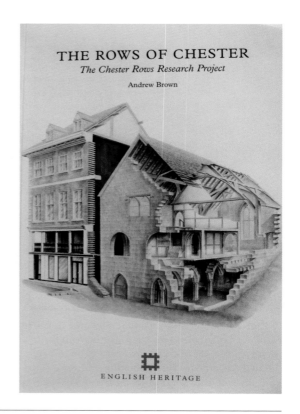

THE ROWS OF CHESTER
The Chester Rows Research Project

Andrew Brown

ENGLISH HERITAGE

English Heritage Commissioner Loyd Grossman and Andrew Brown at the launch of the Rows Study Report.

steps and bridges. But misunderstandings about rights and responsibilities were tackled through the enactment of the Cheshire County Council Act 1980, which set out a clear legal framework, and through the initiation of a programme of repairs to steps and walkways. In 1984, conscious of the need to understand more about the Rows and their origins, it was decided to carry out a comprehensive survey of all the buildings in the four main streets. This project, which was funded principally by English Heritage and the Royal Commission on Historical Monuments, with a contribution too from the Chester Civic Trust, was directed by Andrew Brown, Chester's Conservation Officer, and Rick Turner, County Archaeologist. The research and fieldwork resulted in an archive and a summary report which has informed all subsequent development of the area.

The programme adopted for the Albion Street Action Area was very different, but was also significant in national terms. This small neighbourhood of Victorian terraced houses in the south eastern sector of the walled city had survived largely untouched into the 1960s, but was surprisingly described in the Insall report as being at the end of its life and therefore recommended for replacement with new flats and maisonettes.

Continued on page 89→

Albion Street: a rare example of an intact group of Victorian terraces sympathetically restored.

1987 Blue Coat School railings

The Blue Coat School in Upper Northgate Street dates from 1717 and is one of Chester's finest listed buildings. Modifications in the mid-19th century respected its distinctive Georgian style; sadly this was undermined in the Second World War when the decorative iron railings which enclosed the forecourt were removed for the 'war effort' (little of the resulting metalwork was ever used for the purpose it was intended!).

In 1984 Chester Civic Trust began to look for a project to mark its Silver Jubilee the following year. It was suggested that replacing the missing cast-iron railings would be an important first step in the improvement of the forecourt as a whole. The Trust set aside £3,500 of its own funds but initial estimates for the work, including paintwork and repairs to the stone plinth, came to over £8,500. Chester City Council was keen to include improvements to the paving on the forecourt and this increased the estimate to £11,500.

By October 1985 the Council confirmed a 25 per cent grant offer in addition to the 15 per cent already offered by English Heritage. Both were welcome but they still left an uncomfortable shortfall.

Meanwhile, Roy Archer, chairman of the Trust's Projects & Improvements Committee had the further complication of obtaining permissions from Cheshire County Council and the Chester Blue Coat Church of England Education Foundation, tenants and landlord respectively. Eventually, in June 1986, with permissions granted and a revised budget agreed, the Trust gave the go-ahead for the railings to be made.

Deva Forge of Hoole Bank, Chester, manufactured the railings and gates *"to resemble as closely as possible those erected in 1854"*. The railing heads (or 'spears') were chosen from a range made by A Ballantine & Sons Ltd having regard to their historical authenticity and the safety of anyone attempting to climb over them!

In spite of the grants which had been received, the Trust had to spend more of its own money on this project than it had intended. It politely declined to include the forecourt paving and, to save money, members of the Trust painted the railings themselves in the autumn of 1986.

The President of Chester Civic Trust, The Duke of Westminster, unveiled a bronze plaque at an opening ceremony on 28th April 1987. ■

Members of Chester Civic Trust painting the new railings at the Blue Coat School. Kneeling is Jackie Leech, with Eileen Willshaw, Alison Dodd, Mike Scammell, Jim Sherwood and Brenda Wakeman.

As a result , the houses, which were largely privately owned, were blighted and neglect set in. During the 1970s, when commercial development threatened to cross the inner ring road (there was even a proposal for a bridge across Pepper Street), it looked as though the area might succumb to offices. But by the end of the decade, an increasing regard for the townscape quality of the area led to a re-evaluation, and to the reversal of the clearance policy. Since the houses were not listed, it was realised that renovation would almost certainly result in the loss of external character with a mix of modern windows, plastic rainwater pipes and rendered facades. Thus, in 1981, when the Action Area covering 69 houses was declared, a package of associated measures was introduced to protect its architectural unity. These included an 'Article 4 Direction', giving the City Council control over external alterations, and a design guide explaining the features that contributed to their character for use by house owners. Home improvement grants were supplemented by conservation grants which covered the additional cost of restoring external features such as patterned brick, panelled front doors, sliding sash windows, chimneys and ogee section cast iron gutters. Even the telephone wires and TV cables were undergrounded to avoid unsightly wires and satellite dishes. As a result Albion Street survives as a rare example of an intact group of Victorian terraces.

In the glare of professional scrutiny, questions were sometimes asked about the conservation programme. An article in the *Building Trades Journal* of June 1984 criticised the methods used in some of the Lower Bridge Street projects. Problems arose on the site adjoining Shipgate Street, where the City Council had to serve a High Court Order to halt work on Georgian buildings, and the builder was subsequently fined for demolishing the façade.

Continued on page 92→

A steel frame supports a replica façade in Lower Bridge Street.

1989 Restoration of the snuff mill water wheel

As with many environmental improvement projects, the first hurdle is to establish ownership of the site. This was certainly the case when Chester Civic Trust began to express concern for the derelict water wheel at the weir in Handbridge. The Trust's honorary secretary, Denys Goose, wrote to Chester City Council in November 1982 pointing out *"the poor condition"* of the wheel which by then had fallen over and lost many of its paddles. The letter concluded with an enquiry about ownership. A similar enquiry was made to the Chester Archaeological Society. A prompt response from the Council suggested that the Trust should approach the Welsh Water Authority. So began a protracted period of correspondence in which the water authority, the Council and Tarmac Housing Division (developers of the nearby Salmon Leap flats) all denied ownership, and responsibility! Eventually, in June 1983, after "a very thorough search" of the Deeds in their possession, the Council conceded that they were, after all, the most likely owners. Progress!

At this stage the Trust had no appetite to undertake or manage the restoration itself. Efforts were made to persuade Welsh Water to include the water wheel in a general maintenance project taking place on both sides of the Old Dee Bridge, but whilst the water authority was sympathetic it also raised a series of technical difficulties. Financing the work was another problem and so, for various reasons, little progress was made until early 1987.

In the meantime the Civic Trust had completed the replacement of the Blue Coat School railings and its new chairman, Jackie Leech, generated fresh interest in the water wheel. She took the project to heart and, with her legendary tenacity, set about raising funds and finding organisations that were capable of doing the work. It was a great step forward when, in January 1988, Cheshire County Council's 'Community Programme' agency agreed to manage the work and act as 'contractor'. The Trust was the 'employer': contracts were signed, budgets approved, and work started on site in May 1988.

It was Jackie's ambition that such projects would involve young people. This was soon achieved when the restoration of the water wheel became an 'Employment Training Scheme' (in the Youth Opportunities Programme). These schemes gave work experience and practical skills to

Water wheel in disrepair.

Restoring the water wheel.

young unemployed people for modest remuneration.

Jackie recalled one particular young man who bitterly resented being used, in his opinion, as *"cheap labour"*. He clearly didn't want to be there but, when the job was finished, he admitted to her that he was proud of his involvement and would, one day, bring his own children to see what he had done. Success!

All in all, 16 trainees worked on the project. *"We started with a virtual wreck"* said Geoff Cawley, Project Manager for Cheshire County Council, *"there were just a couple of paddles left, the steelwork was rotten and sections of the retaining wall had fallen in"*.

Work was completed in January 1989, after which a plaque was unveiled by the Trust's President, The Duke of Westminster, on 21st April that year.

Funding came from Welsh Water (£2,500) and Chester City Council (£2,700), with smaller contributions from the Trust's own

funds and The Ancient and Worshipful Company of Drawers of the Dee (one of Chester's medieval guilds).

The only disappointment in an otherwise successful project was that 'for health & safety reasons' the wheel had to be fixed in position rather than allowed to rotate. ■

Jackie Leech and Stephen Langtree inspect the completed water wheel.

The resulting development was a replica façade with a steel frame behind. Further up the street, a largely 19th century half-timbered façade was suspended in mid air on scaffolding whilst the remainder of the structure was demolished, then attached to a new steel frame that was erected behind it. Was this example of blatant facadism taking conservation too far, the author asked, when it might have been better to accept defeat and build anew rather than perform such contortions? (See also photographs on page 58).

Other façades have been retained and restored and the buildings behind adapted or rebuilt.

(Right) a view from the Eastgate of the WH Smith façade in Foregate Street during reconstruction work. (Below) Chester Library: the restoration of the terracotta façade of the former Westminster Coach and Motor Car Works on the Town Hall Square by Cheshire County Council. The building received a Civic Award in 1987 for the restoration and for the interior which reflects the dominant, arched elements of the façade.

Yet these are minor points of concern considering the scale of the conservation programme and the complexity of the task. In 1985 Donald Insall recalled his early visits and the 'dreadful feeling of despair and uncertainty' that he found. Whilst he thought Chester was basically sympathetic to conservation – the Nine Houses, for example, had been restored – he felt the latent opportunities had not really been recognised by local people. His central aim had been to strengthen and reinforce Chester's essential character, which he felt depended on the three most characteristic elements: the Rows, the Walls and the riverside. 'There is no such thing as instant conservation', he cautioned, and from the start of the action areas programme, efforts were made to spread prosperity from the south-eastern quarter, containing the Grosvenor Precinct, back along the streets from which the vitality had been drained.

Conservation in Chester, published by the City Council in 1988, was intended as a guide to help other authorities nationwide. This revealed that over 20 years, 600 buildings had been conserved at a cost of £10 million, half that sum coming from city and government grants, with vital support from the Department of the Environment and later English Heritage. Property values had increased to justify the level of investment, jobs had been created and confidence in the city had risen. In a remarkable spirit of consensus, the expenditure of public funds had never been a political issue, and enjoyed the support of both public and councillors.

In its approach to conservation, Chester pioneered an alternative way of developing a historic city. It showed that fragile buildings need not be sacrificed to the pressures of modern living. The sensitive mix of historic buildings and

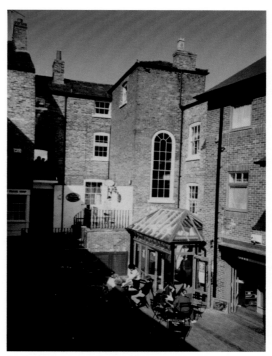

Rufus Court, Northgate Street.

new small-scale developments is another of its most impressive achievements, together with the treatment of open space. Typical of this thoughtful approach is Rufus Court, developed with dogged determination by local developer Rod Cox, with architects James Brotherhood Associates, on land owned by the Dean and Chapter behind Northgate Street. In other places car parking is tucked away unobtrusively to allow for pocket-sized landscaped areas, often paved in historic materials, whilst the tight grain provides a sympathetic setting for both new buildings and old. Donald Insall was the inspiration behind such schemes, where he described his personal philosophy as acting as a kind of doctor, encouraging the self-help of a patient working for his own recovery to health. His aim was to awaken and reinforce the natural ability of a city to guide its own destiny and, during this vital era in the life of Chester, the city moved forward with renewed confidence. ■

1985-98 National Environment Week

Launched in 1985 by the national Civic Trust and other environmental charities, this initiative sought to *'encourage everyone to make a real effort to involve themselves in their local environment .....'* Chester Civic Trust joined in rather tentatively at first but, as with other activities, momentum gathered quickly and Environment Week soon became an important feature in its annual calendar of events. By 1989 the programme of events for members had grown to include visits, talks and, most importantly, practical projects. Visits were made to recycling plants and waste tips, sewage works, quarries, airfields and industrial sites.

A visit to the site of the Manchester Airport second runway was one of several events linked to the theme of transport during Environment Week in 1998.

Clean up campaign along the canal corridor in 1989.

'Grave Concern' - Removal of saplings and undergrowth from the Overleigh Cemetery in 1994. Len Morgan and Suzie Williams with other members of the Trust.

Practical projects have involved many enthusiastic members of the Trust, achieving positive results and good publicity. They have included clean up campaigns along the canal corridor and riverside, the removal of saplings and undergrowth in the Overleigh Cemetery and a challenge issued by Flookersbrook residents to help them paint a mile of railings in one day! Another particularly successful campaign was the 'Graffiti Blitz' in 1990. Working alongside members of the Trust, cleaning and painting walls in Bridge Street and Old Hall Place off Watergate Street, were some of the youngsters who had caused the graffiti. (Their co-operation would, it transpired, be taken into account by the Magistrates when their cases were heard).

Helping Flookersbrook residents paint a mile of railings in one day in 1992. From left, Sheila Gibson (kneeling), Alan Comyns, Richard Hore, Suzie Williams (kneeling), Jan Hore, Daphne Comyns and Stephen Langtree.

Extensive areas were treated with a graffiti resistant paint purchased with donations from local traders. Chester City Council, which supported the project throughout, subsequently introduced its 'Graffiti Busters' cleansing team and Chester Civic Trust was rewarded with a top prize of £1,000 in the national 'Operation Eyesore' competition. ■

Buildings of Chester

During Environment Week in 1995 Graham Fisher (left), Vice President of the Civic Trust, gave a lecture on 'Black and White Framed Buildings of Chester'. With him are (from right), Suzie Williams, Pat Barry, Rita Vokes and Jan Hore.

Cleaning up the vandals' acts...

CONSERVATIONISTS have launched an attack on graffiti vandals with a spring clean blitz.

A 30-strong team from the Civic Trust was joined by Kim Thompson and other members of the City Council's conservation section to tackle graffiti blackspots as part of the programme for Environment Week.

Four young boys, caught red-handed by police painting on walls, joined the clean-up team which concentrated mainly on the Rows.

Stephen Langtree, secretary of the Trust, and the organiser of the graffiti blitz, said: 'It turned out to be a bigger job than we originally anticipated, but simply removing the existing graffiti would have been a relatively short-lived improvement.

'The decision to re-paint the walls with special paint was only possible with generous co-operation from the property owners involved, but we hope it will prove to be of lasting benefit.'

He added: 'We cannot pretend that what we have done will stop graffiti, but the Civic Trust has tried to set an example which we hope will encourage everyone to help keep the situation under control.'

Civic Trust volunteers launch their attack on the City's graffiti. (2660G23A)

Graffiti Blitz during Environment Week 1990.

EIGHT Boom time in Chester

During the late 20th century, Chester's role as a sub-regional centre was a stimulus for job creation, and in 1985 after an intensive campaign, the City and County Councils successfully achieved development status for the city, largely on the strength of its proximity to areas of high unemployment such as Ellesmere Port and Birkenhead. This brought eligibility for government grants, and enabled the district to attract inward investment. To meet demand and to exploit funding for the establishment of business parks, the Councils looked to develop sites on the edge of the city for service employment.

New sites were established on the west of the city along Sealand Road, including the Chester West Employment Park, an 84 acre site which attracted the Chester Chronicle printing works and offices for Pearl Assurance. More significant was the privately owned Chester Business Park,

Chester Chronicle Printing works, Sealand Road.

opened in 1988 on 150 acres south of the city off Wrexham Road. The catalyst for commencement of development was the decision by Marks and Spencer to base its charge card operation there in an impressive purpose-designed building by Aukett Associates. At the same time, Shell Chemicals moved its UK offices from Trafalgar Square in London to the Chester Business Park, though its architectural contribution, in contrast with M & S, was

Marks & Spencer Financial Services, Chester Business Park, Wrexham Road.

The 'Dark Row' scheme in Eastgate Row North was closely based on a proposal by Chester Civic Trust in response to an earlier planning proposal.

Within the city centre, retail interest remained strong with the arrival of Habitat, B&Q, Next and an extension of the BHS store. Perhaps the most challenging scheme was the opening up of the 'Dark Row', the section of Eastgate Row North closest to The Cross, which was designed with appropriate sensitivity by the Biggins Sargent Partnership. On part of Associated Lead's 15 acre site close to Chester Station, North West Securities, now part of HBoS, erected a bulky brick clad office block, whilst the ugly Boughton Retail Park provided premises for Carpetland and Queensway. Ranking of UK shopping centres in a survey by Newcastle University and Hillier Parker in 1984 placed Chester 14th, up from 34th in 1971, the biggest increase for the size of centre. Opposition to a proposal to expand Chester's retail centre yet further, and plans to roll back the green belt for additional employment and housing development were two of the biggest campaigns waged by the Chester Civic Trust at the end of the '80s.

a bland two storey brick box with a false Mansard roof designed by Leach Rhodes and Walker, and described at the time as 'rather like a monster size executive home'.

Office development on the former Leadworks Site near Chester Station.

The retail scheme was the ill-judged 'High Cross' proposal for land at Commonhall Street, behind Bridge Street and Watergate Street. Designed for AMEC by BDP, it took the form of a huge covered mall set at 45 degrees to the Roman street pattern, with an underground service bay and car park for 600 cars in an area of archaeological importance. It was incompatible with the Local Plan objective of small scale shopping and housing improvement. It also involved the demolition of two Row buildings, nos. 28 and 40 Bridge Street and other residential properties.

A developer's exhibition with a glitzy model was upstaged by the Chester Civic Trust which prepared its own planning brief and had a summary printed in the local newspaper. Demolition of the two Row properties was effectively halted by a government decision to spot-list them, and when the planning application came up for consideration by the Council's

40 Bridge Street, one of the two buildings which were spot-listed.

Development Committee, the scheme was unanimously dismissed.

Continued on page 101→

The 'High Cross' proposal for land behind Bridge Street and Watergate Street.

1988-89 Commonhall Street campaign

The 'High Cross' proposal for Commonhall Street aroused almost unprecedented emotions in the city. Labour's planning spokesperson, Councillor Christine Russell, described it as an *"atrocity"* and the local newspapers were inundated with letters.

Chester Civic Trust led a robust campaign against the plans, producing a draft development brief which received equally wide publicity.

The document, produced by James Latham, John Tweed, Michael Scammell and Stephen Langtree, recognised the development potential of the Commonhall Street area and laid down constructive guidelines, generously illustrated with photographs and plans.

"This is not an alternative scheme" wrote Stephen Langtree, the Trust's honorary secretary, *"but a thorough analysis of the sensitive townscape issues which must be respected in any future plans"*.

Over 100 copies of the full-colour brief were produced and widely circulated. The media campaign against the 'High Cross' application reached national proportions but Chester Civic Trust's positive contribution in the form of the 'Commonhall Street Brief' is thought to have tipped the balance.

The 'High Cross' application was unanimously rejected by Chester City Council and a few weeks later, in February 1989, Stephen Langtree received a letter from HRH The Prince of Wales endorsing the stance taken by the Trust. ■

A draft planning brief was prepared by Chester Civic Trust.

The conflict over the green belt, named by the Daily Telegraph as 'The Battle of Chester' was more drawn out. This arose over a proposal included in the draft Local Plan for the removal of 1,000 acres of land from the green belt for development. At a public inquiry into the plan in October 1988, the Conservative controlled City Council argued that Chester could not continue to prosper either in its own right or as a generator of regional prosperity without such a release of land. For the government, and in particular the ideologically-driven Environment Secretary Nicholas Ridley, the issue posed a dilemma. In Ridley's view, places like Chester, that had the appeal to attract business from more prosperous parts of the country, offered an opportunity to challenge what he saw as simplistic talk about the North South divide. Over the previous four years businesses had been relocating to Chester rather than moving away, particularly with the incentive of grant aid, and with this influx had come a demand for housing. House prices had been rising by 30-40% in a single year, and the two Councils felt it was important to broaden the economic base away from an over-reliance on tourism and associated service industries to achieve long term stability.

Lined up against the proposal was the CPRE (backed by the Chester Civic Trust), which argued that the rural setting of Chester was as important as its historic monuments and physical fabric, and to allow the proposal would undermine a founding principle of green belt policy which was to preserve the special character of historic settlements such as Chester. It was widely seen as a test case for other northern and midlands conurbations, and between the opposing parties there was no consensus.

Six months later the Inspector's report was published; he concluded that no exceptional circumstances had been demonstrated for such large scale development proposals, and added that the alterations to the green belt boundary would have an adverse effect on the character of the historic city. However, his recommendation that the proposals be dropped was not binding on the City Council, which decided to proceed regardless, and the plan was duly referred to the new Environment Secretary, Chris Patten. At this point, Stephen Langtree, who had recently taken over as Secretary of the Chester Civic Trust, wrote to Patten pointing out that whilst there may be an understandable temptation to capitalise on the relative success of historic towns and cities and allow expansion, the ensuing pressures from unprecedented growth may seriously compromise or even destroy the identity of places like Chester. His point was that the cold analytical assessment of planners and economists that Chester is a sub-regional centre did not fairly represent the full value of the place and its community. There was a real danger that potential visitors and businesses could be deterred by over congestion of roads and suburban sprawl around the city. After a lengthy period of deliberation, in July 1990, the Secretary of State announced his 'decision'. It was to prevent the Council from formally adopting the plan until he had completed his assessment of the Cheshire Structure Plan, which was due to be considered at an Examination in Public in October of that year. The only way the City Council could have avoided a further lengthy hiatus was to drop its proposals for the release of green belt land, which it was not prepared to do.

Continued on page 103→

1992 Commemorating Chester's Lord Mayoralty

In April 1992 Her Majesty the Queen visited Chester to distribute the Royal Maundy at a service held in Chester Cathedral. At a ceremony later, in the Town Hall Council Chamber, Her Majesty granted Lord Mayoralty status to Chester, and Councillor Susan Proctor thus became the City's first Lord Mayor.

To commemorate the City's new status, Chester Civic Trust decided to present a coffee table for the Lord Mayor's Parlour in the Town Hall. Designed and made by Roy Archer (then vice chairman of the Trust) in his furniture workshop at Aldford, the table is of American walnut inlaid with rosewood and boxwood. The table was presented to the City's second Lord Mayor, Councillor John Randall, by Mrs Gertrude Jones, a founder member, past Chairman of the Trust, and at that time the Trust's senior vice president. Recalling the long association between the City Council and Chester Civic Trust, she expressed the hope that they would continue to work closely together for many years to come. ■

Presentation of the coffee table: (left to right) the Lord Mayor of Chester (Councillor John Randall), Roy Archer and The Duke of Westminster.

The immediate reaction from councillors was frustration, Christine Russell, Chair of the Development Committee, claiming that the delay posed a 'major threat to the city' when it had only recently been awarded development area status. The Council remained adamant that development on the periphery was essential to take the heat off the historic city centre and promote a healthy local economy, and if expansion could not go on the city fringes, it would have to go to the surrounding villages.

The final decision on both the County and City Council's plans fell to Michael Heseltine, who returned to his former post as Environment Secretary in John Major's government after the downfall of Margaret Thatcher. In 1992, he decided to block development of 800 acres of green belt land, which meant that the business park proposal at Mannings Lane, the 900 home development at Wrexham Road and housing development at the Countess of Chester Hospital were all shelved. Heseltine reduced the city's housing requirements from 7,800 to 6,100 and its industrial land target from 210 hectares to 100. The Chairman of the County Council's Environmental Committee accused him of 'locking up jobs in a cabinet at Whitehall', and jeopardising some 17,000 jobs in Cheshire in the run up to the end of the century. Heseltine's justification for the decision, however, was a fear of overdevelopment, and in order to explore the issue in a practical way he asked both Councils to join with English Heritage and his department in the preparation of an 'environmental capacity study', the first such analysis to be applied to a historic town.

The capacity study, which was carried out in two parts by consultants Arup Economic and Planning and Building Design Partnership, found that visitor numbers were nearing saturation point, which threatened the pleasure of being in the historically rich environment. By measuring walking speeds, pedestrian numbers and traffic flows the consultants found widespread evidence of tensions, caused by 'competing demands for the limited street space at the heart of the city'. The purpose of the study was to assess what development Chester could realistically sustain without further erosion of fabric and loss of character, and a set of 'capacity guidelines' were assessed, relating to such pressures as green spaces, townscape, urban grain, archaeology and historic buildings. The intention was to establish a level at which capacity may be reached and not be exceeded, so that taken together, these guidelines might form a framework for measuring the environmental capacity of the historic city. The challenge for the City Council was establishing what planning options might be devised that would allow the city to maintain its sub-regional role without exceeding the capacity threshold. As a result the next version of the Local Plan took a very different direction. ■

1994 The Civic Award Scheme – one small step remembered

In 1979 Chester City Council had inaugurated the Civic Award Scheme as a contribution to the celebrations of the 1900th anniversary of the foundation of the city in 79AD. Whilst the scheme followed the pattern of the well-established national Civic Trust Awards, it had the intention of attracting entries which would not necessarily have been submitted to or be recognised in a country-wide award scheme.

The Awards were both popular and successful. They were repeated in 1984, 1987 and in 1991 but it was not until 1994 that Chester Civic Trust joined with the City Council and the Cheshire Society of Architects to promote the scheme for the fifth time. The occasion was the 25th anniversary of the publication of the Insall Report. As the Trust's newsletter noted, it was also 25 years since a man had set foot on the moon for the first time, but it had been the Insall Report rather than the moon landing which had made the headlines in the local press in 1969. The moon landing may have been, in the words of Neil Armstrong, *"one small step for man, but one great leap for mankind"*, but the Trust recognised that the Insall Report has been an important first step in launching the city's conservation programme.

Since 1994 Chester Civic Trust has continued to play an increasing role in the organisation and administration of the award scheme. The scope of the scheme has continued to develop and expand and, in addition to rewarding the best architectural projects completed within the previous five years, the publicity which the awards attract has undoubtedly raised the profile of good architectural design in the city.

The Magistrates' Courthouse was one of the award winners in 1995, the assessors describing it as "an outstanding example of a truly modern building fitting well into the conservation area". Since this photograph was taken insensitive alterations have been made to the entrance steps.

The City Council's plaque for the inaugural awards in 1979 featured the profile of Vespasian, the emperor of Rome in 79AD.

Plaque for the awards in 2000.

The eighth award scheme was, appropriately, held in 2010, the Trust's Golden Jubilee year; it included the extended area of the new Cheshire West and Chester Council and, in addition to the three sponsors, the Council, Cheshire Society of Architects and Chester Civic Trust, received national recognition for the first time with support from English Heritage. The awards were presented by the Lord Mayor, Councillor Neil Ritchie, at a ceremony in the Town Hall which attracted an audience of over 200 architects, contractors and owners whose projects had been nominated.■

Civic Award winners in 1995.

1988-89 'Places for People'

In 1988 the North West Civic Trust launched an award scheme for civic and amenity societies with the dual purpose of rewarding and publicising exceptional activity. Jackie Leech, Rhiannon Bentall and Stephen Langtree submitted a document on behalf of Chester Civic Trust and were awarded second prize (£300) – beaten on this first attempt by Buxton Civic Society.

The following year the Trust tried again with even more to report, including their fight to protect the Green Belt, and the Commonhall Street Development Brief. This time the Trust was the outright winner, receiving a certificate and a cheque for £500. ■

Stephen Langtree, Rhiannon Bentall and Graham Fisher collecting First Prize in the 1989 'Places for People' presented by Stuart Hall at the BBC Studios in Manchester.

1989 Shopfront Design Awards

Shopfronts are always changing: sometimes the new design, colour scheme and signwriting are sympathetic and successful, but sometimes they are not. The latter stand out like the proverbial 'sore thumb', especially when seen in the context of Chester's traditional 'black & white' architecture.

In 1989 the Trust decided to run a competition to find the best (and worst) shopfronts in the city centre. Organised with the Chester Chronicle, nominations were invited from Trust members and the public. Dozens were received, giving the judging panel, chaired by Graham Fisher, quite a task. Laura Ashley in Eastgate Street Row was awarded first place, four shops were highly commended. Two received a 'wooden spoon'! This popular competition was sadly not repeated until the advent of the Trust's 'New Year Honours' in 2007. ■

Penhaligon's (Eastgate St Row) was 'highly commended' along with Liberty (Bridge St), Hatchards (Watergate St) and Warehouse (St Werburgh St).

1994 YMIR is unveiled in Grosvenor Park

The tactile sculpture of Ymir, a Norse mythological figure representing the Source of the World, was commissioned by Chester Civic Trust in 1993 to mark the Cheshire Celebration Year of Culture. Financial support was received from Cheshire County Council, Chester City Council and MANWEB (the regional electricity board whose headquarters were based in Chester).

Situated in the Garden for the Blind in Grosvenor Park, the sculpture was the culmination of an initiative by the Trust two years earlier to promote a sensory garden. Designed and created by Phil Bews, Ymir was unveiled by The Duke of Westminster, President of Chester Civic Trust, in September 1994.■

Ymir: public art commissioned by Chester Civic Trust.

The Duke of Westminster unveiled Ymir in the Grosvenor Park (left to right) Roy Archer (chairman, Chester Civic Trust), The Duke of Westminster and the Lord Mayor of Chester (Councillor Gordon Smith).

NINE A right old carry-on

At the same time that the future of the green belt was being debated, another controversial planning proposal in Chester was exciting national as well as local interest. This was a scheme put forward by local businessman Tony Barbet to excavate and partially reconstruct the amphitheatre as a visitor attraction to be known as *The Deva Roman Experience*. The scheme, which was the subject of a public inquiry in early 1988, involved the demolition of Dee House, a Grade II listed building that stands on top of part of the amphitheatre, to allow for full excavation of the site, together with peripheral activities such as galleys plying the River Dee and a café selling 'Roman' food. It divided the heritage sector: archaeologists generally supporting the application, whilst historic building professionals were determined to retain the Georgian Dee House. The City Council came out in favour of the scheme, as did English Heritage, which promoted the archaeologists' line at the inquiry in support of the proposal.

The architectural correspondent, Gavin Stamp, who gave evidence against the scheme on behalf of the Georgian Group, wrote a piece in the Daily Telegraph entitled *A right old Roman carry-on*, with an illustration of Sid James in Roman centurion's armour accompanied by his co-star Julie Stevens wearing very little.

Sketch of proposed Deva Roman Centre on the site of the amphitheatre.

Stamp claimed that the City Council wanted the scheme because it was jealous of the success of the Jorvik Centre in York and was desperate to attract more tourists to Chester. He castigated archaeologists for their assumption that ancient monuments were more important than standing buildings, and felt that such thinking gave heritage a bad name. Indeed, as he pointed out, a backlash against conservation had already begun to be heard, as exemplified by the influential book *The Heritage Industry* which had recently been published. In this book the author Robert Hewison saw a growing national obsession with the past as a disturbing counterpart of economic collapse. Instead of manufacturing goods, Hewison argued, the country was obsessed with manufacturing heritage, a commodity that no one was able to define, but everyone was keen to sell. Stamp regarded the hypothetical reconstruction of 15% of the amphitheatre, the foundations of which would destroy any real Roman remains, as a falsification of the past, and *The Deva Roman Experience* as an attack on real heritage. When the Secretary of State's decision on the application was announced in June 1988, it transpired that the Inspector had recommended that it be refused, but Nicholas Ridley disagreed and granted consent.

Any euphoria created by the prospect of a tourist attraction in the city to rival the Jorvik Centre, however, was short-lived, for by May 1990 the *Deva Roman Experience* was in financial trouble. With the original backers having withdrawn, and no other companies prepared to invest in the project, Barbet lost his option to purchase the site, and it was another ten years before the future of the amphitheatre was once again to be seriously considered.

One of the conditions placed on the planning consent for the amphitheatre project was the provision of a park and ride service linking it with an enlarged car park at Chester Zoo, for concerns about the continuing increase in traffic dominated planning debate at this time. In 1990 the City and County Councils jointly released for public consultation the *Chester Traffic Study*, which aimed to change the public attitude to private and public transport so as to meet the needs of the 21st century.

Continued on page 112→

Public consultation on the Chester Traffic Study.

1996 Finding a home - Bishop Lloyd's Palace

For many years Chester Civic Trust held its committee meetings and conducted business from members' homes. In the early 1970s a generous legacy left by Mrs Millicent Hartley was believed to be for the purpose of enabling the Trust to acquire an office and a base for its activities. Unfortunately, Mrs Hartley's Will was not explicit and many members preferred to carry on as before rather than risk the financial stability it had given the Trust.

By the mid-1980s, however, the need for a base was becoming increasingly evident. Stephen Langtree, the Trust's new honorary secretary in 1987, recalls how quickly his house was over-whelmed with Civic Trust files and paperwork!

Early plans included a serious proposal to set up an office in the rooms above the Abbey Gateway. Practical problems, not least difficult public access, hampered this plan but the vision was now well established. Space was found at No 8 Abbey Square where the Trust 'opened for business' in May 1992. Small fund-raising events were held on and off the premises to defray the cost of renting the room.

In April 1994 Chester Civic Trust moved to 126a Northgate Street but it was clear by then that, even with a favourable rent, premises that did not generate income would be a continuing drain on the Trust's financial reserves. It was equally clear that the Trust needed premises where members could meet and where the Trust could invite the public to call and find out more about the civic society movement. The City Council was approached with a view to the Trust taking a lease on the main rooms in Bishop Lloyd's Palace in Watergate Street.

Bishop Lloyd's Palace, Watergate Street.

This was eventually achieved in 1996 but only after prolonged negotiations regarding the lease. Honorary secretary, Jan Hore, recalls the sterling work of many volunteers which enabled the Trust's new headquarters to be up and running in time for Heritage Open Days. In previous years the Trust had opened the building on behalf of the City Council. Now the Trust could, for the first time, welcome members and the public to see its own premises. Jan Hore also recalls how the building was adapted for its new purpose and how it was achieved:

"With advice from James Latham, we converted the Ladies cloakroom into a small office and a store room next door became the new Ladies WC. Suzie Williams applied a coat of paint to the office walls; Richard

Hore fitted a carpet donated by the chairman Roy Archer, Stephen Langtree designed a desk and shelves to maximise the use of the rather limited space while Peter Brigham, vice chairman, arranged the donation of bookshelves. Then, with the help of several members, we cleaned the rooms from top to bottom and moved our existing furniture from Northgate Street".

For the last 16 years the Trust has occupied the historically important part of this early 17th century timber-framed building in the heart of Chester. Listed Grade I, it has fine carvings on the gable elevation and at Row level. The interior includes magnificent period fireplaces and highly decorated plaster ceilings.

In 2002 the Trust embarked upon a major scheme of interior repairs and refurbishment. Designed and supervised by Donald Insall Associates, with financial help from the Heritage Lottery Fund and Chester

City Council, the work included new heating, re-wiring, new carpets and curtains as well as repairs to many historical features.

Bishop Lloyd's Palace has proved to be an excellent setting for Chester Civic Trust, raising its profile in the local community and providing an income for the Trust through the letting of rooms. ■

The interior is remarkable for the oversized fireplaces and overmantles and the ornate plaster ceilings.

Proposed light rail transit system.

The main elements of the study were the introduction of a light rail transit (LRT) system, expansion of park and ride, additional pedestrianisation, segregated bus lanes, and a circular cycle route. The LRT was the most radical proposal, the first stage of which was intended to link Chester Zoo with Foregate Street, following a disused rail track initially, and then continuing on lines set into the city roadways.

A modest Park and Ride scheme had been operating from Sainsbury's on the eastern edge of the city since 1983. Although at first opposed by the Conservative group, which was worried that it would incur

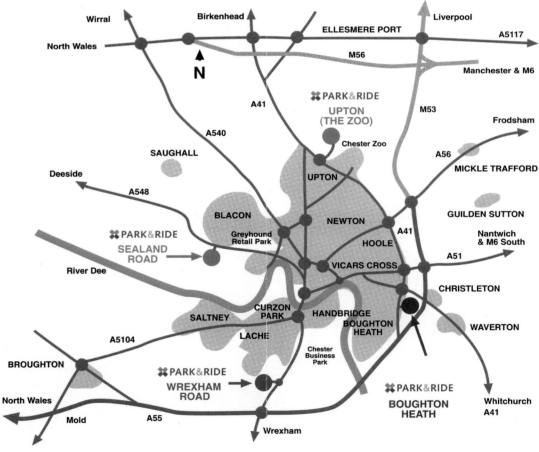

Plan of Park and Ride Sites.

Proposed extension of the pedestrian area.

Further pedestrianisation was proposed for Bridge Street, Watergate Street, St Werburgh Street, St John Street and parts of Frodsham Street, whilst the closure of Eastgate Street and Northgate Street was to be brought forward by one hour. In addition, buses were to be banned from St Werburgh Street and Eastgate Street. Unlike other historic towns such as York and Oxford, cycling was never especially popular, and the plan was intended to encourage more bicycle usage by creating a circular route based on canal towpaths, closed river frontages and little-used city centre roads.

losses for the City Council, the service soon proved popular and was successful in reducing the number of cars entering the city centre. In time it was accepted that even if it would never be self-financing, Park and Ride represented the most economic means of reducing congestion in the city, and a 'car parking facilities fund' was set up to provide finance for future car parking initiatives, with a levy of 10p coming from every car using the city centre car parks. Thus the 1990 traffic plan proposed an ambitious target of 4,000 car spaces by 2005, to be provided on six separate sites around the city edge. Restricting all the car parks within the inner ring road to short stays was intended to act as a further disincentive to bringing cars into the centre.

The final and most problematic element of the plan involved the completion of the outer ring road to take stress off the Grosvenor Bridge and open up the western side of the city. Whilst the north western section had been completed through the release of land at the Greyhound Park for retail development, funding for the south western section, with a new crossing of the River Dee, was dependent on the release of land in the green belt. In its scope and ambition, the plan represented the first attempt to co-ordinate all the city's traffic problems and find common solutions. Over time certain elements such as park and ride, cycle routes and bus lanes were implemented; others like the LRT system proved to be too expensive, and were dropped.

The early 1990s, however, was a period of economic recession, and before the general loosening of financial constraints allowed the implementation of public works such as the street improvement programme, Chester had suffered severe spending restraint. The recession had also led to a number of business closures including retailers such as Fred Cowley and Queensway Stores, and the cancellation by Owen Owen of plans to extend their premises on Bridge Street. A major development proposal for land at Mercia Square between Frodsham Street and the City Wall was abandoned, leaving a prime site totally cleared and surrounded by ugly hoardings. Old established firms such as the 194-year-old Hydraulic Engineering Company in

Charles Street and Sothebys Salerooms also closed during the recession.

Another casualty of belt tightening was the Conservation Programme, which was cut by 75 per cent to a mere £50,000 in 1992/93, with jobs in the conservation team being lost or frozen. In real terms the money available for the maintenance of historic fabric and the enhancement of conservation areas was lower than at any time since the Fund had been set up in December 1969. *'We cannot sit back and witness this decline without protest'*, commented the Chester Civic Trust. The County Council, for its part, decided to close the St Mary's Centre, abandoning its acclaimed environmental education programme and thus denying school

Perspective by S H Tasker of Building Design Partnership of a proposed scheme to replace the former Mercia Square development between Frodsham Street and the City Walls: one of several projects in the city which did not materialise. This scheme would have maintained the link with Frodsham Street and the City Walls.

St Mary's Centre (the former Church of St Mary-on-the-hill) - Gouache painting by Richard Hore.

children the opportunity to benefit from the facilities that had been developed at the former church. Ironically, these decisions came the year after the City and County Councils had jointly received the prestigious Europa Nostra Award for the second time, only one of two places in Europe to be honoured in that way. ∎

St Mary's Centre was a valuable education resource for schoolchildren.

⛫ Out and About

From the formation of Chester Civic Trust in 1960, visits by members to other towns and cities have been an important feature of the Trust's calendar. They have provided the opportunity for members to see and understand the problems faced by other towns, to learn about their solutions and to enjoy both old and new buildings.

The first visit, in July 1960, was to Coventry. The highlight was a guided tour of the then recently completed cathedral, followed by a walk around the city centre led by a member of the City's Planning Department.

Since then half-day and day visits have been made by coach on a regular basis, extending in 1990 to a weekend in Kingston-upon-Hull and in 1995 to Europe to visit Chester's twin town of Sens in France. On many of the visits the Trust has been able

Dublin, 1991: Chester Civic Trust's first flight.

to meet members of local civic societies and has reciprocated hospitality when civic societies have visited Chester.

In an article in 2001 Stephen Langtree, then Chairman of the Trust and a founder member of the North West Association of Civic Trust Societies commented on the *"helpful and friendly reception members*

Swansea, 1998.

Belfast, 2008.

of the Trust had received from local civic societies" and continued *"we always find that we have a lot in common. We share many of the same concerns and aspirations; we promote many similar issues; we campaign for similar improvements; and we can learn a lot from each other's experiences."*

Guinness is good for you? Limerick, 2001. From left, Greba Donaldson, Stephen Langtree and Muriel Greenwood.

Chester Civic Trust now runs a variety of trips every year, ranging from half-day visits to nearby villages to four or five-day visits abroad. In 2011 the programme included Stoke-on-Trent, Cambridge and Berlin. Their success is due to careful planning by Pat Barry, Jan Hore and Gillian Fisher, and their popularity, according to Stephen Langtree, is that *"they retain that special Civic Trust ingredient which is altogether more rewarding than a conventional holiday!"* ∎

Berlin, 2011.

TEN Ambitions for the 90s

Following Michael Heseltine's decision to protect the green belt and keep a tight cap on any physical expansion of Chester's boundaries, the recession provided the opportunity to take stock and consider what the city's role might be when the recovery came. Reacting to the Secretary of State's decision, Stephen Langtree called for a review of potential development sites within the existing urban area, highlighting vacant or semi-derelict areas such as parts of Canalside in Boughton, Seller Street and Egerton Street, Gorse Stacks, Commonhall Street, and the Royal Infirmary. In 1993 the Chester Action Programme was established, consisting of more than 300 public, private and voluntary organisations. Its aim was to ensure a co-ordinated approach to urban development, and 200 projects were planned over a three year period tackling regeneration in the city and making use of under-utilised areas. The programme included the establishment of a City Centre Manager, jointly funded by the public and private sectors, action on homelessness and affordable housing, and improving visitor facilities. The protection, maintenance and enhancement of the historic and natural environment were recognised as key objectives of the action plan.

The biggest project was the proposed remodelling of the Forum by Scottish Widows. A scheme by the previous owners Legal and General Assurance Company had been aborted after English Heritage forced a call-in by the Secretary of State. The new scheme, designed by Leslie Jones and Partners of Manchester, was at first restricted to the addition of a small department store for T J Hughes and an extension of the retail area facing Town Hall Square. This involved the creation of a new glazed frontage in place of the overhanging office block. However, the completed scheme failed to conceal what remained of the original structure, and was condemned by the Chester Civic Trust as *'superficial, facadist and motivated more by commercial considerations than by civic pride'*. The next phase was more ambitious – it was intended to double the retail floor space as well as provide a new market and bus exchange – but perhaps fortunately, like the Legal and General scheme, it too was soon abandoned.

Another ambitious but abortive proposal was the 'Millennium Wall', a bid made by the City Council to the National Lottery Millennium Fund for a 21st century section of city wall to be erected along the line of the inner

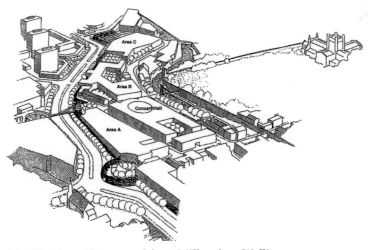

The City Council's proposal for a 'Millennium Wall'.

1993 The remodelling of The Forum

When the planning application to partially demolish and re-face the Forum was submitted, Chester Civic Trust considered that the proposal represented a wasted opportunity to revive the civic and cultural heart of the city. In the view of the Trust, the re-modelling was little more than cosmetic surgery, Chester was in danger of replacing one mistake with another, a prediction which was well-founded. ■

ring road between Northgate and the Bars containing a new cultural quarter. This visionary scheme met with a mixed response – Stephen Langtree spoke for many when he remarked *'I have to confess I am very doubtful about its success'*- and indeed it failed to get through the first lottery fund sift. But undaunted by this experience, the Council, supported by the Chester Civic Trust and other partners, embarked on an imaginative proposal for an Architectural Lighting Strategy with the aim of securing Heritage Lottery Funding.

The contrast between Chester's day and night time ambience had long been a source of concern, for the post war population decline in the city centre and the limited range of evening activities had made many of the streets unwelcoming and even threatening after dark. The impetus for the lighting project came through an invitation from the Trust to the respected lighting consultant Andre Tammes to deliver a public lecture on the subject of illuminating historic towns. Following his visit, the project swiftly gained momentum and, underpinned by 'seed-corn' funding from MANWEB, an integrated lighting strategy for 'the city within the walls' took shape. This was supplemented by an assessment of how the scheme might be used to benefit the local economy. The ideas were well received by the local community, and celebrated by local school children, whose imaginative paintings gave a dazzling impression of Chester's potential night time appearance. In 1996 a bid was submitted to the HLF for a pilot project that would serve to demonstrate how historic places could be sensitively and efficiently lit at night, an issue that was a subject of considerable national debate. It therefore came as a deep disappointment when, after a very long delay, the HLF Trustees, whose resources were then under pressure, decided the scheme could not be considered a priority.

Without lottery funding, the strategy could never be completed in its entirety. Whilst a few elements, such as a sympathetic lighting scheme for the Rows walkways, were implemented, in the absence of a new and different approach to street lighting and for illuminating landmark buildings, the opportunity to give the city a distinctive night-time appeal was lost. The failure to carry out the scheme, which won the Parliamentary Lighting Award in 1998, was a major set-back during the period that turned out to be the final and late flowering phase of Chester's acclaimed conservation programme.

For, during the later 1990s, in spite of the reduction in the conservation fund, which was never reinstated, the conservation team was to embark on a number of public works projects that greatly enhanced the character of the city centre. Funded partly by capital loans from government, many of these schemes were related to LODIS, the European transnational co-operation project, which Chester devised and led with funding from the EU. This imaginative project, in which the Chester Civic Trust was a local partner, was aimed at demonstrating how local distinctiveness could contribute towards economic competitiveness. Under the co-ordination of Chester's conservation officer, the six partner municipalities (Visby in Sweden, Salerno in Italy, Catania in Sicily, Vale do Lima in Portugal and Limerick in Ireland) carried out a diverse range of pilot projects. In Chester, pedestrianisation was expanded,

Chester's plans for a high-quality architectural lighting scheme received the All-Party Parliamentary Lighting Group's 'Leading Light Award'. The award was a working replica of the first practical electric light bulb demonstrated by Sir Joseph Swan in 1879. At Westminster for the award presentation were (from left to right) Stephen Langtree (Chairman of Chester Civic Trust), Christine Russell MP, Gerry Halas (Managing Director of Scottish Power), Tony Baldry MP (co-chairman of the All-Party Parliamentary Lighting Group) and Peter de Figueiredo (Head of Conservation and Design for Chester City Council).

A view from the Eastgate: work in progress on the high quality street paving.

of the Town Hall Square, the commission of a bespoke suite of street furniture, interpretation of the Rows and a public art programme were never fully progressed. Yet this was a pro-active period for conservation, and if some projects were not followed up, the reason was that Chester's ambition often ran ahead of its ability to deliver. Determined to maintain and enhance its position as an international tourist destination, the City Council and its partners were never short of ideas. This sometimes led to expectations that could not be fulfilled. The most significant project that has so far failed to happen is the transformation of the amphitheatre from a semi-circular grassy slope dominated by a high retaining wall into a visitor attraction of international interest.

Continued on page 126→

and a programme of high quality street surfacing was carried out in Bridge Street, Watergate Street, Eastgate Street and Foregate Street using natural stone in a simple manner that set new standards for the treatment of the public realm in a historic city centre. An innovative waymarking and interpretation scheme was introduced to encourage use and enjoyment of the City Walls. Another scheme involved the provision of surface crossings of the ring road as an alternative to the unpopular subways; one of the crossings helped the regeneration of Brook Street which had previously been cut off from the centre. But in time resources ran out, and proposals for the redesign

One of the interpretation plaques on the City Walls.

1993 - 2000 Seeing Chester in its best light

It was on a cold, dark November evening in 1993 that lighting consultant André Tammes of Lighting Design Partnership transcended the gloom with a stunning vision of how our towns and cities could look at night. Invited by Chester Civic Trust's chairman, Stephen Langtree, Tammes addressed a joint Civic Trust meeting with 'Presenting Chester' partners. His case for an integrated 'Urban Lightscape' strategy involving buildings, open spaces and landmark features was well made and illustrated with individual examples from the UK and Europe.

The enthusiasm engendered by the lecture led to the Trust becoming the catalyst for action and, over the next two years, a comprehensive feasibility study was undertaken. A partnership was formed to promote the architectural lighting strategy, including the City and County Councils, City Centre Management Panel and Chester Civic Trust together with MANWEB, CEWTEC and other organisations.

By the end of 1996 two major studies had been completed with sponsorship from MANWEB and ABSA (the Association for Business Sponsorship of the Arts),

The Chester Civic Trust

LECTURE SERIES 1993/94

Joint Meeting with 'Presenting Chester'

Tuesday 23rd November

'THE URBAN LIGHTSCAPE'

Andre Tammes
(Director of Lighting Design Partnership, Edinburgh)

An illustrated talk which focuses on the underexplored area of the night-time perception of our cities and towns. Andre Tammes will argue for strategic lighting planning, reviewing individual city projects while setting the subject within an international context.

The Grosvenor Museum 7.30pm

ADMISSION

MEMBERS - Free;

NON-MEMBERS £1.50

PRESENTING CHESTER

A PARTNER IN THE

CHESTER Action PROGRAMME

supplemented by grants from the City and County Councils and Chester Civic Trust. The first was a technical feasibility study undertaken by Lighting Design Partnership in association with Donald Insall Associates. The focus was to be the *"City within the Walls"* using lighting

Feasibility Study for lighting the City Walls and Old Dee Bridge.

Presentation of 'Pride of Place' awards by The Duke of Westminster. The Civic Trust received the award in recognition of the outstanding contribution that the Trust had made to the Architectural Lighting Scheme for Chester.

sparingly but effectively to create an inviting night-time ambience. The second study was an economic impact assessment, a unique exercise in terms of architectural lighting, undertaken by the European Institute of Urban Affairs at Liverpool John Moores University.

The partnership was further encouraged when a study tour was made to Lyon in France where the investment in lighting their buildings, open spaces and bridges, had been rewarded by a revival in its tourist industry.

Throughout this period the Trust was assiduously represented by Stephen Langtree and Cyril Morris and, after an on-site demonstration in the city centre was planned for early in 1997, Stephen Langtree

declared that *"we have the technology and the expertise – all we need now is the money"*!

Far from being an utopian dream it was a practical, fully developed and fully costed strategy with demonstrable economic benefits as well as improved safety and security – and a significant reduction in light pollution. The Trust's representatives continued to promote the scheme through the City Council's Steering Group and an application for funding a first phase was made to the Heritage Lottery Fund.

REVEALING CHESTER'S HERITAGE
AN ARCHITECTURAL LIGHTING SCHEME FOR THE CITY

Rows lighting, Bridge Street East.

With such momentum and expectation it was extremely disappointing for all those who had worked so hard on the project since 1994 when, in June 1998, the HLF Trustees decided that they could not support the application. Hopes had been high that, with a first class study backed up by an economic appraisal of the benefits and supported by publications by the Royal Fine Art Commission and the Institution of Lighting Engineers, Chester would be at the forefront among historic cities. It was a small consolation that the HLF Trustees noted the thoroughness with which the scheme had been prepared and that the professional team appeared to be experienced and capable of delivering a complex and innovative project.

Despite the disappointment, the strategy received national recognition in December 1998 with the "Leading Light Award" from the All-Party Parliamentary Lighting Group. A further award followed in May 1999 when Chester Civic Trust received the City Council's first "Pride of Place" award *"in recognition of the outstanding contribution that the Trust had made to the Architectural Lighting Scheme for Chester"*. Receiving the award from The Duke of Westminster Stephen Langtree said *"We are delighted to receive the Award .... but the only reward we really want is to see the lighting scheme being fully implemented across the whole City"*.

Meanwhile, a reduced scheme to light the Rows and key sections of the City Walls was prepared by the Trust and the City Council, the City's Conservation Officer, Peter de Figueiredo, commenting that *"To see the Walled City subtly and carefully lit would give a different feel to the City at night"*.

Above: Rows lighting - Watergate Row North.
Below: (from left) Christine Russell MP, Howard Dickenson
(City Council Design and Conversation Manager) Stephen Langtree
(Chairman Chester Civic Trust) and the Lord Mayor Councillor
Eric Plenderleath at the launch of the Rows Lighting project.

Only the Rows Lighting Scheme was implemented with support from Osram and designed by Lighting Design Partnership (by then Lightmatters). The comprehensive relighting of the Rows, highlighting the architectural features with specially designed downlighters and wall lights, was completed in 2000 and formally launched at a reception hosted by the Trust at Bishop Lloyd's Palace.

Ten years later Chester Civic Trust still retains the enthusiasm and ambition for Chester to become the most beautifully and sensitively lit historic city in the country. ■

REVEALING CHESTER'S HERITAGE
AN ARCHITECTURAL LIGHTING SCHEME FOR THE CITY

Following the collapse of the *Deva Roman Experience* in 1990, the site remained dormant, with Dee House boarded up and unused. Although the management of the excavated part of the amphitheatre was transferred from English Heritage to the City Council, nothing was done to improve the presentation of the monument. Then in 1994 an opportunity arose. BT indicated that it wished to sell Dee House and its grounds, together with the 1920s office building behind, which also stood on a part of the amphitheatre, and urged on by the Chester Civic Trust, the City Council opened negotiations to acquire the site and reunite it with the excavated part. Unfortunately the Council was unable to finance the purchase, and entered a partnership arrangement with David McLean, a local housing developer, whereby his company would acquire the rear section of the site including the 1920s building, whilst the Council would take Dee House. But by this time English Heritage had changed its stance and not only opposed the demolition of Dee House, but also favoured preservation rather than excavation of sensitive archaeological sites. For this reason the Council was reluctantly obliged to consider retaining the listed building and converting it into an interpretation centre.

Again funding was the obstacle, and whilst the City Council struggled to find a way to move forward on Dee House and the excavation of the amphitheatre, David McLean applied for permission to replace the 1920s building with a new headquarters for his own company on the same footprint. Although planning consent was granted in 1995, work never commenced, and after several years, during which the future of the amphitheatre continued to be a subject of keen public debate, it was thought that the scheme had been abandoned. It therefore caused consternation when in early 2000, just as planning permission was due to expire, it was announced that McLean had reached agreement with the Court Service and the County Council to build a new County Courthouse on the site. Furthermore, permission had been granted to vary the 1995 planning consent without reference to city councillors or the general public.

During this time public opinion had strengthened for the total excavation of the monument and its display as a major tourist attraction, and the action of the Court Service was seen as a betrayal of trust. Stephen Langtree captured the public mood in a letter to the Lord Chancellor appropriately entitled

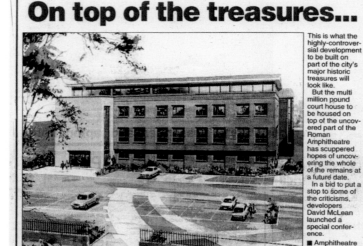

On top of the treasures...

This is what the highly-controversial development to be built on part of the city's major historic treasures will look like.

But the multi million pound court house to be housed on top of the uncovered part of the Roman Amphitheatre has scuppered hopes of uncovering the whole of the remains at a future date.

In a bid to put a stop to some of the criticisms, developers David McLean launched a special conference.

■ Amphitheatre special: Page 4.

An artist's impression of the courthouse which was built over the uncovered part of the roman amphitheatre.

Visitors from near and far

Bishop Lloyd's Palace has provided an ideal venue in which to welcome visitors to Chester and introduce them to the work of the Civic Trust.

Many visiting groups have been civic societies from this country but one of the most memorable groups came from Shirakawa in Japan. Their first visit, in 1994, was arranged by the British Council following the designation of their village as a World Heritage Site

The village is notable for distinctive thatched roofed houses in a style known as Gassho because they are said to resemble the appearance of hands in prayer. The steeply sloping roofs help to shed snow which covers the village for three months of the year. World Heritage status has led to an influx of visitors during the summer months and an inevitable conflict with farming activities and the normal life of the village.

Members of the Trust were able to explain the work of a civic society and how the village might benefit from a similar organisation. They were also introduced to the concept of Park-and-Ride as a solution to the increasing number of visitors arriving in cars.

Their first visit was such a success that they asked the British Council to include Chester and the Civic Trust in each of their subsequent four visits to this country! Peggy Grimshaw, a Civic Trust member and Blue Badge Guide, proved to be so popular that each group would ask, through their interpreter, *"Where is Mrs Peggy?"*. Copious notes were made to be shared on their return and so their annual study programmes were expanded to include the Friends of the Meadows, Queen's Park Residents Association and the role of a Conservation Officer.

A reciprocal visit to Shirakawa by Civic Trust members has not yet been arranged … but, maybe, one day?! ∎

'A Monumental Injustice', and in July 2000 more than 500 protestors, organised by the Chester Amphitheatre Trust, brought the city to a standstill in a campaign to halt the construction of the Court House. The media covered the story almost every week for six months, with articles published in national and local newspapers and interviews conducted on TV and radio. Yet construction of the courthouse continued, whilst English Heritage, fearing criticism, tried its best to remain disengaged. Caught off balance, the City Council launched a comprehensive public consultation exercise, but by 2002 the court was in use, and Langtree expressed his frustration, observing that 10 years after BT decided to sell Dee House, re-igniting the debate about its future and what lies beneath it, all that was to be seen on the site was a semi-derelict listed building and a new courthouse which should never have been built, and may shortly have to be demolished if the amphitheatre was to fulfill its potential. The divergent views between the City Council and English Heritage on the future of Dee House also heralded a significant deadlock. ∎

1994 Heritage Open Days

CHESTER DISTRICT

Heritage Open Days
11th ~ 14th September 2008

CELEBRATING 40 YEARS OF CONSERVATION IN CHESTER

HERITAGE OPEN DAYS
8 - 11 SEPTEMBER 2011

The Chester Civic Trust

Cheshire West and Chester

alled garden.
hurs 9th to Sun 12th
dnight. Please visit
w.oddfellows.biz fc
ormation. Wheelch
n rear via Grosver

St. Mary's Cen
Mary's Hill
erly the church
-on-the-Hill.Cor
0 partly to serv
ing needs of t
ester Castle, a
Victorians. N
ents. Cheste
e Volunteers
otographic d
History & H
and Sat 11
0 to 4.00pm
air access.

egate F
Place,
ridge St
orgian hc
ilding, n
ward winning
n architects Donald
ciates. Contains a
fine staircase.
of building with
ion of Donald Insall
rojects.
urs at 10.00am &
king essential on

Thurs 9th - 12 noon to
11.30pm, Fri 10th and Sat 11th
12 noon -to midnight. Sun 12th
12 noon to 11.00pm. Limited
wheelchair access (with one
step) to the ground floor.

20. Off the Wall,
12 St. John Street

In 1990 Chester Civic Trust had made their first weekend visit, to Hull, where the local civic society already opened buildings not normally open to the public. The idea was brought back to Chester and tried as part of the Trust's Environment Week programme.

The Heritage Open Days were part of a Council of Europe initiative co-ordinated in England by the national Civic Trust and supported, at that time, by the Department of National Heritage. In 1994 Chester Civic Trust joined in the national Open Days held on the second weekend in September, opening Bishop Lloyd's Palace to the public free of charge. Negotiations between the City Council and the Trust for the lease of Bishop Lloyd's Palace had begun but were not to be concluded until 1996. In the meantime the Trust's volunteers helped to

Brochure covers (left) the Eastgate by Donald Insall and (right) the Interior of St Paul's Church, Boughton by Richard Hore.

welcome visitors and serve refreshments. As Suzie Williams wrote in the Trust's newsletter: *"The response from the public was astounding. Over the two days we opened the Palace for eleven hours. During that time over 900 visitors passed through! We were inundated with people of all ages and nationalities. They were eager for information about the building and about ourselves … It really was an amazing success and a great encouragement for our negotiations with the City Council to take over the running and letting of the building".*

Suzie, then Jan Hore followed by Peter Bingham and Christine Robinson have all been champions of Heritage Open Days over the years. The number of buildings open to the public during the September weekends has gradually increased and has been supported by the local authority and, more recently, by English Heritage following the demise of the national Civic Trust.

The launch of the Open Days in 2008 celebrated the 40th anniversary of the Insall Report when many of the buildings restored during the conservation programme were opened to the public.

In 2010, the Trust's Golden Jubilee Year, Heritage Open Days were expanded across the new borough of Cheshire West and Chester. The well established partnership between Chester Civic Trust and the Council continued in association with Tarvin Civic Trust and with support from English Heritage; 50 buildings were opened to the public free of charge. In addition a number of walking tours and events were arranged with help from several local societies throughout the new local authority area. Chester Civic Trust also produced 'A Golden Jubilee Selection' of buildings completed between 1960 and 2010. Many of the 26 buildings identified were to open to the public during the weekend.

Heritage Open Days have been one of the 'success stories' of the Trust and Chester now has one of the largest programmes anywhere in the North West. Whether it is curiosity or a deeper appreciation of architecture, the public enjoys seeing the interiors of buildings which have usually remained unseen. Nationally, it has been said to be the biggest free celebration of England's architecture, history and culture. ■

The national launch of Heritage Open Days in 2008 was held at Chester Racecourse and commemorated the 40th anniversary of the publication of the Insall Report (left to right): Christine Robinson (Chairman of Chester Civic Trust), Donald Insall and Cyril Morris.

ELEVEN The new Millennium

The economic upturn of the late 1990s and the early years of the new Millennium provided the background to Chester's next phase of development. Since the rejection of the two Councils' plan to roll back the Green Belt around the city, work had continued on a new Development Plan for the whole district, setting out a framework for development up to 2011. The emphasis on sustainable development through integrated land use and transportation planning reflected new government priorities and differed markedly from the previous expansionist strategy. Development was to be contained within the existing Green Belt until 2011, and growth was to be managed by holding back development of the Sealand Basin until the Western Relief Road was built.

The Scout Headquarters in Tower Road received a Chester Civic Award in 2000.

The development in New Crane Street retained a fragment of the Chester Electric Lighting Station façade.

The plan encouraged development of 'brownfield' before 'greenfield' sites, and an emphasis was placed on public transportation with the construction of eight new park and ride sites and the introduction of a guided bus system in line with the earlier *Chester Traffic Study*.

The first of the strategic regeneration areas to be planned was the Old Port which was given impetus by being included in the West Chester Single Regeneration Budget programme. This included the land to each side of New Crane Street, bounded by the river, the railway viaduct and Tower Wharf. Phase 1 involved social housing around the canal basin and a boat-shaped Scout HQ, both designed by Tweed Nuttall Warburton. The most interesting project, a competition winning design by Manchester architects MBLC for an office building on New Crane Street, was abandoned in the face of public opposition to the loss of the Electric Light Company offices that stood on the site. The mediocre development that eventually took place, by other architects and retaining a mere fragment of the original Electric Light Company frontage, was a poor compromise. As Langtree commented at the time, echoing James Chandler's earlier beliefs, *'I am increasingly convinced that the secret of successful conservation is a skilful blend of the new and the old'*.

Planning Briefs were also produced for the development of the Boughton Canal Corridor, the Railway Lands north of the station, the Police HQ, the River Corridor, Tower Wharf and Gorse Stacks. During 2000 and 2001, numerous planning applications were submitted for apartment schemes in the city centre, including the Leadworks, Looker's Garage at Hoole Lane, the Royalty Theatre on City Road, and the former Chester Hydraulic Engineering Works at Egerton Street. In an attempt to bring greater coherence to this densification of the city, the Chester Civic Trust decided to set up an Urban Design Panel to respond to the plethora of briefs, transport plans and policy initiatives. They also arranged a 'Round-the-Houses' open-top bus tour of the developed sites to assess the state of progress.

At the same time, redevelopment of the Forum came back onto the agenda. In 1999, planning consultants Donaldsons were asked to prepare a development brief for what was now called the Northgate area, for which the City Council was seeking a development partner. The following year a competition was held, which was won by developers London and Amsterdam (part of Dutch bank ING) with Michael Hopkins Architects. It was immediately apparent that this was a scheme of much higher quality than those that had previously been worked up for the site. But it was also much more ambitious: at a cost of £185 million, it was the largest redevelopment scheme ever seen in Chester, with a huge department store, 60 additional retail units, a new market hall, a multi-storey car park and housing. The Chester Civic Trust had concerns, firstly with the immense scale of the development, but also with the transport arrangements and the loss of the library, which was to be replaced with a new facility at first floor level above the shops. Yet it was generally recognised that the scheme offered very positive advantages: the dismal legacy of the 1960s, including the despised Commerce House, was to be replaced, and Chester's cultural life was to be re-invigorated by a new venue to replace the ageing and inadequate Gateway Theatre. The historic street plan of the area was to be reinstated, with elegantly designed contemporary retail units on two levels in emulation of the Rows, and a new enclosed square providing the setting for the theatre was to be formed. The Town Hall Square was to be redesigned and freed of clutter. One uncertainty was the future of the City Council's offices, for whilst it was resolved that they would have to move off the site, it was not clear at that time where they might go.

In 2003 the Northgate planning application was submitted. By this time the scheme had expanded yet further, taking in all the land between the backs of Watergate Street and Hunter Street. The Chester Civic Trust was generally supportive, believing it would bring lasting benefits for the city in terms of new employment opportunities, improved public facilities and new residential properties. The City Council's surprising proposal for new offices, however, provoked a storm of protest.

Continued on page 136→

Artist's impression of proposed new elevation to the Town Hall Square including a new street in line with the west front of Chester Cathedral.

Artist's impression of proposed Performing Arts Centre in the south-west corner of the redevelopment site.

2000 'Forty Years Young'

More than 100 members of Chester Civic Trust assembled in the Blossoms Hotel on 7th January 2000, appropriately on the same date and in the same place as the public meeting at which the Trust was formed in 1960.

As on many anniversaries there was a sense of both nostalgia and achievement. The Lord Mayor, Councillor Eric Plenderleath, referred to the *"robust opposition"* of the Trust to inappropriate developments coupled with their *"equally positive ideas for improvement"*. The chairman, Stephen Langtree, was congratulated by the Member of Parliament, Christine Russell, for leading the *'2000 Years of Building'* Millennium Celebration.

One of the guests was Professor Quentin Hughes OBE MC, a founder member of the Trust and its chairman from 1963 to 1966. James Latham recalled the appointment of Quentin Hughes by the City Council to co-ordinate the improvement schemes in the city's central streets. He observed that, in the mid 1960s, the scheme had made a huge difference: in his opinion, it marked a turning point in the City's morale.

With no fewer than six other past-chairmen present, it was a good opportunity to reflect on the Trust's history since 1960, but the over-riding mood was one of anticipation. It was, after all, only seven days since the new millennium had been heralded in with firework displays and parties all over the

Past chairmen of Chester Civic Trust: (front row L to R) Professor Quentin Hughes, Dr Allan Pullin, Dr Rosemary Martin and John Maddock. (Back row) Jackie Leech, Graham Fisher and John Wakeman with Stephen Langtree (Chairman in 2000).

world. Perhaps Trust members were relatively unmoved by the media hype, but their own Millennium Festival was only just getting started. Within two weeks the Millennium Lecture Series was underway with Donald Insall addressing an audience of over 300 in the Town Hall. Evidence, if needed, that Chester Civic Trust was 'Forty Years Young' and still going strong! ■

Quentin Hughes cuts the anniversary cake with Stephen Langtree, the Trust's longest serving Chairman. Quentin Hughes was a founder member of the Trust and responsible for the Bridge Street Improvement Scheme. He had won two MCs whilst serving in the SAS and later made a notable reputation as a conservation architect. He was actively involved in the Trust's activities until he left Chester in 1968 for Malta to set up a School of Architecture at the Royal University.

Having made the decision to move its offices out of Northgate, the Council pinpointed Gorse Stacks as a suitable location. Whilst the Gorse Stacks Brief had stimulated private sector interest in developing the upper part of the area by the Northgate roundabout, the lower end had less appeal. This was a challenging site, long and narrow, and within the sight line of an important view of the Cathedral Tower from the approach to the city centre. Acting on the advice of Andy Farrall, Director of Development, the Council commissioned the celebrated but controversial Manchester architect Ian Simpson to design the new building, His proposal was uncompromisingly modern: a fully glazed, free-form structure rising to six storeys, which was swiftly nicknamed 'the glass slug'. After much debate, the Trust decided to support the scheme – their letter described it as imaginative and unmistakably modern rather than elegant or beautiful – and with English Heritage and CABE also in favour, the Council bravely approved it by nine votes to three, in spite of hostile public reaction. In the rapidly changing economic climate after 2005, however, the cost of relocating the Council's offices was one of the factors that caused the redevelopment of the Forum once again to flounder.

By 2005 the city centre housing boom had reached its climax. One of the earliest and largest schemes was the development of the site of the Royal Infirmary by Jane Darbyshire and David Kendall for Bryant Homes, which was completed in 2002. This created 100 new houses and apartments in a well-landscaped layout between the ring road and the City Wall (the original 1761 Infirmary building was retained and converted to apartments).

Continued on page 142→

The proposed council offices at Gorse Stacks ('the glass slug').

The listed Chester General Infirmary building on City Walls Road has been restored and converted into luxury apartments.

The St Martin's housing development on the former Royal Infirmary site.

2000 Celebrating the Millennium

In the year 2000 Chester Civic Trust was 40 years old and the city, founded by Imperial Rome in the first century AD, was almost 2000 years old. It seized this coincidence as an opportunity to plan and deliver an ambitious year-long Millennium Festival, **2000 Years of Building**.

Conceived and promoted by Chester Civic Trust the festival was delivered through an active partnership with the City Council, local architects and the Chester College of Higher Education, and with generous financial support from the Heritage Lottery Fund and the President of Chester Civic Trust, the Duke of Westminster. Following a popular programme of activities including a lecture series representing each of the centuries in the two millennia, two main

2000 YEARS OF BUILDING
A Festival for the Millennium

CELEBRATING CHESTER'S DEVELOPMENT THROUGH TIME

outcomes continue to highlight Chester's unique legacy of buildings and structures. The first is an architectural guidebook: *2000 Years of Building – Chester's Architectural Legacy* published in 2001. The second is Chester's Millennium Festival Trail: a

Promoting the Festival in Feb 1999, Stephen Langtree (Left) is joined by the Trust's principal patrons - Eileen Willshaw (Chester City Council), Gary Bubb (Cheshire Society of Architects) and Professor Graeme White (Chester College - now The University of Chester).

Launch of Millennium Festival Trail: (left to right) the Lord Mayor of Chester (Councillor Reggie Jones), Council Leader Councillor John Price (standing) Christine Russell MP and Stephen Langtree (Chairman of Chester Civic Trust and of the Millennium Festival Partnership).

three mile city walk covering 40 of Chester's buildings that represent the city's development through time. The public selected the buildings as outstanding examples of Chester's architectural development. Each is celebrated on the ground with its own unique marker created by artist Michael Johnson.

139

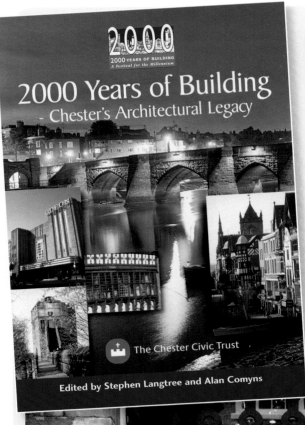

Other aspects of the Millennium Festival included an education programme involving hundreds of local schoolchildren, a photographic competition, a travelling exhibition and a very large model of a Rows building which was the centrepiece of a highly successful exhibition at the Grosvenor Museum. In total the Festival had a turn-over of £86,000, involved dozens of local organisations and was, by far, the biggest project ever undertaken by the Trust. ■

"2000 Years of Building – Chester's Architectural Legacy" celebrated both the city's millennium festival and the 40th anniversary of Chester Civic Trust. Pictured at the launch of the book at Bishop Lloyd's Palace are (from left to right) the Duke of Westminster, Dr Alan Comyns, Stephen Langtree, the Lord Mayor of Chester (Councillor Graham Proctor), Dr Peter Bingham and Christine Russell MP.

Part of an extensive (8 feet high) site hoarding painted by local schoolchildren.

(Above) Stephen Langtree and Tom Hand launching the travelling exhibition which toured the country.

(Right) Poster for the Grosvenor Museum exhibition.

The same architects designed a contemporary scheme for Wimpeys at The Bars. Whilst these two projects were designed to relate to the density of surrounding development and respect their historic setting, some of the schemes that followed appear to have been driven solely by commercial considerations. In the Chester Civic Trust newsletter of August 2004

The Grosvenor Court offices at the east end of Foregate Street.

it was observed that new apartment blocks were exceeding the recommended densities set out in the City Council's planning briefs, whilst many of the capacity limits set in the briefs had been disregarded. Pointing out that privately-owned green spaces were also being built on, large gardens were being infilled and bungalows on the approach roads to the city such as Lache Lane and Hoole Road were being replaced by blocks of flats, Stephen Langtree asked rhetorically whether Chester's residential building boom was producing anything to be proud of.

Now that the boom has passed, and the developments can be looked at more dispassionately, positive results can be found. The residential population of the city centre has grown significantly and some areas of previously shattered townscape, particularly along the edges of the ring road, have been patched up. The brownfield development also reduced pressure to alter the Green Belt boundary as had been intended. The best individual schemes include St Martin's Gate and The Bars, which reflected something of the quality of the well-regarded Grosvenor Court office scheme designed by David Ross for the Stannanought Partnership at the traffic island at the end of Foregate Street in the late 1980s.

New apartments at The Bars.

New apartments on the former Leadworks site.

The first phase of development at the Old Port, and Tweed Nuttall Warburton's housing on the Leadworks site also respond sympathetically to their settings. The remodelling and extension of Jackson Stops' building on Nicholas Street and Alexander Court at the corner of Dee Hills Park and Boughton, both by Ian Simpson make a welcome addition to Chester's scant catalogue of modernist architecture. But the bulk of the projects, particularly those along the canal corridor and at Tower Wharf, are tired variants on the brick warehouse theme or pale imitations of the Vernacular Revival that made such a positive contribution to

Alexander Court, Boughton.

Dee Hills Court, an apartment block overlooking the river Dee which received a Chester Civic Award in 2005.

The Jackson Stops building on Nicholas Street was remodelled and extended.

Chester's cityscape in the late Victorian period. These have irreparably damaged the character of the city. In 2006, the Chester Civic Trust carried out a survey of members' opinion on recently completed projects entitled A Fair Deal for Chester. Twelve schemes, nearly all apartment blocks, were assessed against design-based criteria, and none engendered enthusiasm.

The highest scoring were the Earl's Court apartments at the Old Port, a traditionally styled three-storey block with repeated gables on the edge of the canal link, and Dee Hills Court, a stylish apartment block by Tweed Nuttall Warburton, faced in white render, with projecting balconies overlooking the river. The same architect's Leadworks scheme was placed seventh, and Ian Simpson's Alexander Court, which caused much controversy at the planning stage and was clearly disliked, came second to last. The wooden spoon went to the six-storey Ethos apartment block on City Road, probably the worst of the neo-warehouse style developments, and deservedly castigated.

Earl's Court apartments at the Old Port.

Continued on page 146→

2003 Birthday treat for footbridge

With Environment Week long gone by, but with the satisfaction of undertaking practical projects still fresh in some minds, Chester Civic Trust decided to give the Queen's Park Suspension Bridge a 'wash & brush up' for its birthday! The rationale was that 2003 was the 80th anniversary of the opening of the 'new' footbridge in 1923. A major refurbishment had been completed in the late 1990s but the paintwork had already become dirty - especially beneath the overhanging trees at the south end. Trust members did what they could to clean the parapets; work was necessarily limited to the accessible areas but for a while thereafter the bridge did look better cared for. ■

An 80th birthday present for the Suspension Bridge: the Civic Trust's 'wash and brush up' party (left to right) Cynthia Paley, Richard Hale, Stephen Langtree, Caroline Holton and Suzie Langtree.

West Cheshire College in Handbridge.

The Northgate project was not the only large scale commercial development proposed at this time. There was a £100 million scheme for a Hilton Hotel on the site of the Northgate Arena, with a replacement leisure centre, offices, a new fire station and 700 new homes on land off Sealand Road. The developer behind this project was Steeltower which, like the scheme itself, has sunk without trace. West Cheshire College also had its eye on the Northgate Arena site, seeing the car park there as a potential location for a new campus. This was intended to be funded by the demolition of its existing premises in Handbridge which would be replaced by a housing development. In the face of local opposition, however, the College abandoned the proposal and decided on a more modest project to redevelop its Handbridge site and expand in Ellesmere Port. Mixed use development has taken place in fits and starts at Gorse Stacks to a overall masterplan designed by

Stephenson Bell. Whilst the masterplan was welcomed by the Trust and promised contemporary architecture of high quality, the resulting 'design and build' development, especially the Travelodge Hotel has been disappointing.

A scheme of these years which proceeded to completion through the subsequent economic recession was the redevelopment of the Constabulary Headquarters overlooking the racecourse. A lucrative sale of the Chester site was needed by the Cheshire Police Authority to fund its new Police headquarters at Winsford, and Liberty Properties was selected as its preferred development partner. Using local architects McCormick Architecture, Liberty proposed a drum-shaped building containing a hotel, offices and apartments, set around a central open courtyard. The design, which was said by the architects to have been influenced by Chester's amphitheatre, deviated markedly from the City Council's brief in rising to seven storeys rather than four, and instead of forming a backdrop to the existing cityscape, it was intended to make a powerful architectural statement in its own right. The Chester Civic Trust felt it would dominate the Castle and its setting and prejudice views of the city from Grosvenor Bridge, the river and the Roodee. CABE too was unhappy. But the political stakes were high, and in 2006, in the face of considerable opposition, the scheme was approved. Now the project is completed, it is clear that the Trust's fears about dominance were to a large extent justified. In the important views from the Castle complex, the new building lacks the slim elegance of the Police HQ that it replaced. Yet at ground level the building is much more sympathetic, whilst public access across a site that was previously out of bounds is a considerable benefit. Looking back to the County Council's

The HQ building which replaced the Police Headquarters, viewed from Nuns Road.

efforts to build offices adjoining the Castle Mound in the 1960s, it is ironic that the building has now been let to the new Cheshire West and Chester Council to serve as offices for local government officers displaced from County Hall. As a result, the proposed leisure and cultural uses that had been the principal reason for the central space have been abandoned. Instead of being a lively addition to Chester's public realm, with cafes and restaurants spilling out into a sunny courtyard, the area is now a sanctuary for bureaucrats. ■

Queen Victoria's view of HQ from the Castle Square. Perhaps she was not amused!

2007 New Year Honours

Chester Civic Trust's *'NEW YEAR HONOURS'* were conceived and introduced in 2007 by Stephen Langtree. The idea of an award scheme run exclusively by a local civic society was nothing new but, having chaired the North West Association of Civic Trust Societies (nw.acts) since 2002, Stephen was well aware of the success of such schemes in other places.

It was important, however, to avoid confusion with Chester's 'Civic Awards for design & conservation' which occur every five years under the joint auspices of the local Council, the Cheshire Society of Architects and, since 1995, Chester Civic Trust. So, the new scheme was deliberately titled 'New Year

NEW YEAR HONOURS 2010

The Good, the Bad and t

CHAIRMAN'S SPECIAL A

(new building)

ALL SAINTS CHURCH OF E
PRIMARY SCHOOL, SAU
an exemplary design incorp
highest standards of energy e
sustainability.

The Chester Civic Trust
www.chestercivictrust.org.uk

NEW YEAR HONOURS 2011

The Good, the Bad and the Ugly

CHAIRMAN'S SPECIAL

(leisure faciliti

JOSH'S JUMPS, QUE
VICARS CROSS; Jo an
together with Great Bc
Council have provided t
well used BMX track fo
memory of their

The Che
www.ches

NEW YEAR HONOURS 2012

The Good, the Bad and the Ugly

CHAIRMAN'S SPECIAL AWARD

(building refurbishment and shop fitting)

STEAMER TRADING COOKSHOP;
the rear of the shop opens up into a
delightful light and airy 3 storey space
with a central stair well.

The Chester Civic Trust
www.chestercivictrust.org.uk

Josh's Jumps, Queens Road, Vicars Cross. Jo and Steve Easton, together with Great Boughton Parish Council, provided this BMX track in memory of their son Josh (2011).

All Saints Church of England Primary School, Saughall by Lovelock Mitchell Architects, described as an exemplary design (2010).

Honours' (in deference to Her Majesty's rather better-known awards!) and sub-titled 'The Good, the Bad and the Ugly'. Nominations are invited every autumn in these three categories. They aim to reflect positive changes to the built environment in the preceding twelve months, no matter how small, as well as to reward personal endeavour. Similarly, in the 'Bad' and 'Ugly' categories, local eyesores and deteriorating situations can also be highlighted.

The winners are announced in the New Year. All those in the 'Good' category are presented with certificates at a buffet lunch in the Trust's headquarters at Bishop Lloyd's Palace.

Walker Street Community Park, Hoole, involving local school children (2009).

The New Year Honours have proved to be a very popular initiative. They help to promote better standards of design and maintenance, recognise the efforts of organisations, individuals and community groups and draw attention to some of the things which need to be put right. Moreover, they raise the profile of the Civic Trust – and don't cost much to run! ∎

Cafe and Bistro, 71 Brook Street: a renovated building adding to improvements to Brook Street (2011).

Award winners with the Chairman of Chester Civic Trust, David Evans.

TWELVE Facing the future

The game of musical chairs that has seen Council staff moving around a changing stock of buildings within the city is one of the consequences of local government reform, a topic which has pre-occupied the political elite of the County and City over recent years. The final decision to separate the county into east and west, the latter being given the name of Cheshire West and Chester, was widely perceived as a compromise to satisfy Chester's aspirations for unitary status in its own right. In the lead up to the political changes, a sweeping restructure of the City Council's services saw its delivery arm transferred to a public/private sector partnership known as Chester Renaissance. The Renaissance programme of development and investment, with a total value of £1.5 billion, is intended to run until 2015, and make Chester a 'must-see' European destination. The largest Renaissance project is the Northgate development, currently stalled due to economic uncertainty, though likely to be resurrected shortly in a much reduced form. Another major scheme, the first phase of which has been successfully completed, is the multi-million pound refurbishment of Chester Station and its surroundings. Commendable too are the recent repair and refurbishment of the Town Hall, and the introduction of an enhanced transport service between the city centre and Chester Zoo.

A multimillion pound refurbishment of Chester Station was completed in 2010 and included the lighting of the main facade.

The Roman Amphitheatre: following archaeological excavations recent improvements have included defining the outline of the structure and (below) a mural painting.

In recent years Chester Renaissance has led on the troubled issue of what to do with the amphitheatre. Following two high-profile excavations that produced a new understanding of the history of the monument and its setting, it was agreed to explore practical ways of interpreting the amphitheatre without damaging the archaeology or demolishing Dee House. The scheme that has recently been completed has involved defining the outline of the original structure on the excavated area of ground, and creating an illusionistic mural painting

on the rear wall to provide an impression of the amphitheatre in its full extent. Whilst sensibly avoiding the grandeur of previous proposals, it hardly meets the aspirations of those who saw the amphitheatre as Chester's star attraction, and most visitors remain underwhelmed. The next phase, if funds can be raised, is likely to involve the restoration of Dee

Community events in the amphitheatre.

House as a archaeological museum and a space for the city's Roman collection, ironically a scheme that is similar to one put forward by the Chester Heritage Trust more than 15 years ago.

Whilst public attention was focused on the amphitheatre, some observers noted a worrying drop in the standards of care for other historic sectors of the city. This was dramatically highlighted when in April 2008 a 30 metre section of the City Wall alongside the Grosvenor Hotel collapsed. Throughout their history, the walls have suffered from unpredictable movement; in 1988 substantial stretches of both the north and east walls were taken down and rebuilt because of concerns about their structural condition. But more recently regular monitoring had lapsed, and vegetation had been allowed to grow over the stone surfaces, making it difficult to inspect the condition of the walls. Since the collapse, Chester Renaissance has acted to address these

shortcomings, rebuilding the fallen section, carrying out repairs in two other areas of instability, clearing the vegetation and commissioning a comprehensive structural survey. A study by Donald Insall Associates is also under way with EU funding to find imaginative ways of making greater use of the towers as visitor attractions.

Another area of concern has been the Rows, Chester's most important heritage asset. Management of the Rows is exceptionally complex because of the fragmented pattern of ownership, the unusual arrangement of a public walkway running through privately owned buildings, and the pressure of commercial interests. The fragile nature of the historic structures, the ever-present threat of fire, and the problems of access are other issues of concern. In recent years many traders have disregarded the byelaws and placed sign boards on the Row walkways and streets, and draped banners over the

Chester Civic Trust's 'Public Realm Group' inspecting the City Walls and their environs - (left to right) John Wolfenden, Dorothy Clift, Jennifer Gill, Howard Dickenson (Head of Conservation and Design, Chester City Council), Philip Harrison and Ann Jones.

Repairs to the City Walls south of the Eastgate in 2010.

balustrades of the galleries. The Council's failure to prevent these eyesores from proliferating is a sorry abnegation of their responsibilities, which will make it more difficult to combat clutter in the future. In 2007, a Rows Improvement Campaign was launched by the Renaissance partnership, together with the Chester Civic Trust, and the owners and tenants of Row buildings. Since the campaign launch, standards of cleansing have improved, and the introduction of dedicated community safety wardens has led to a reduction in anti-social behaviour, but the problems of clutter, poor design standards and un-coordinated lighting have yet to be seriously tackled.

Two other historic areas where problems remain are the Castle and the Cathedral Quarter. These are the subject of recent Conservation Management Plans. Like the amphitheatre, the Castle has been an embarrassment for English Heritage, which acts as guardian for the inner bailey with its medieval buildings and castle walls, some of which moulder in a state of neglect. Two of the former Ministry of Defence buildings too, Colvin House and Napier House, have long been empty and in the hands of the Crown Estate. The former parade ground, potentially the most impressive public space in the city, is blighted by use as a car park for staff of the Council, the Crown Courts and the University. Whilst discussions between all the differing public sector landowners have continued over many years on how this historic area could be brought back to life, no agreement has ever been reached on a practical way forward. The recent decision of Chester University to occupy the former County Hall may help to break the impasse and lead to a solution that would benefit the citizens of Chester and the city's visitors rather than the vested interests of the existing owners.

Chester Castle: Agricola Tower.

The Cathedral Quarter too fails to contribute to the life of the city as it should. After a long period of under-investment, where its buildings were allowed to fall into slow decline, the Dean and Chapter have sensibly come to the conclusion that a proactive approach to management of its property portfolio is required. In this case the Management Plan is accompanied by a development strategy. But tensions have arisen between the Cathedral staff who see opportunities for new development on some of the open land and English Heritage which favours a more cautious approach. As a result the development strategy has not been released for public comment, while little has been done to address the high levels of vacancy and poor condition of the wider cathedral estate. Meanwhile imaginative but controversial proposals for a new entrance to the Cathedral and

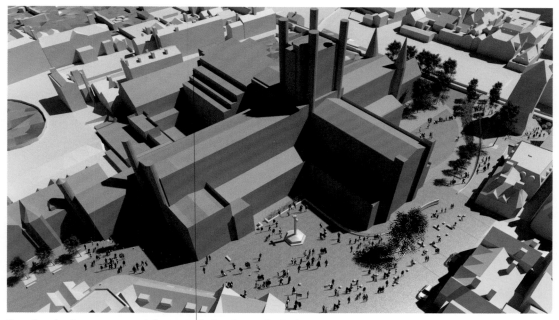

Imaginative but controversial proposals for the Cathedral Quarter.

visitor centre have been dropped in the face of widespread opposition.

The failure to secure investment for the Northgate redevelopment has had repercussions. The new and less ambitious Northgate scheme currently being drawn up is unlikely to include a new indoor market, a theatre or a bus station, and if the city is to retain these facilities, they will have to be accommodated elsewhere. A proposal for a market on the Kaleyards car park has not been well received, since it involves building on an area of land that has been open since the foundation of the city, and conflicts with one of the fundamental principles of the Greenwood Plan. Finding a potential home for performing arts, however, has moved a step forward with the recent and welcome acquisition by the Council of the Odeon Theatre. The future of bus transport in the city centre remains unresolved.

The Northgate scheme was also to have included the redesign of the Town Hall Square, which remains compromised

by through traffic and general clutter. Although there has been no movement on this flagship public realm project, the idea proposed by Grenfell Baines in 1964 for uniting the cathedral and the town by removing the railings along the edge of St Werburgh Street was recently revived. This project, designed by BDP and jointly commissioned by the Council and the Dean and Chapter, promptly ran into trouble, with battle lines being drawn between traditionalists and modernisers. A redesign found favour with the planners and in principle support from the Chester Civic Trust, on condition that the issue of traffic and parking in St Werburgh Street could be dealt with. But with continued opposition from other groups, the Council's planning committee refused consent for the scheme in November 2011. It remains to be seen whether the city will have to wait another half century to see the proposals put into effect.

Continued on page 157→

'Signs of the Times'

For many years Chester Civic Trust has objected to inappropriate fascias and signage, poorly designed shopfronts and hanging signs which do not emulate the traditional wrought iron brackets and hand-painted lettering. More recently, the Trust has drawn attention to the incipient growth of 'A' boards on the streets and banners on the balustrades of the Rows. All of these, the Trust believes, can rapidly combine in a visual shooting match which devalues Chester's townscape and defeats the very commercial ends which they are intended to promote.

The Trust has, however, tried to be positive, encouraging good design of shopfronts through its 'New Year Honours' and assisting the restoration of historic hanging signs. The weakening of legislation and enforcement in the interests of economic development can lead to standards being lowered and the care and attention to detail, so essential in a conservation area of international importance, can soon be eroded. Undoubtedly, this will be a continuing concern for Chester Civic Trust.■

50 years after the foundation of Chester Civic Trust, the future of planning and development in Chester rests in new hands. In all the debates about local government reform that led up to the creation of a unitary Council, the Trust had one principal concern. This was how the new authority would deal with the issue of 'Place'. In recent years, the inter-linked environmental responsibilities of the old City Council – physical planning, regeneration, economic prosperity, housing management, climate change and community safety – became fragmented, not always to the benefit of performance or quality standards. The Trust hoped that this might be addressed in the new departmental structure. Yet in all the consultation and publicity put out by the embryo Council, no mention was made of the importance of the city's unique built environment or the value of safeguarding its architectural heritage. The Trust was worried that the focus of the new authority, with a population three times the size of the old one, and with differing local priorities, would be less disposed to recognise the distinctiveness of Chester's historic city centre. In a continuing dialogue between the Trust and Council leaders, some of these fears have been allayed. The Council has made it clear that one of its top priorities is to gain the belief and trust of the public, and to achieve this objective, the Trust would be invited to engage in early discussions whenever major development projects or significant heritage issues were involved. The Trust too was welcomed as a partner in formulating the new Local Development Framework which would set out the future direction of planning for the District.

In mid 2010, in a frank acknowledgement that the historic city faced serious challenges, the new Council and a number of private sector partners came together to invite the respected Urban Land Institute (ULI) to provide an international perspective on Chester's future. The expert panel's incisive report, produced in November 2010, highlights a number of structural weaknesses in the city's social and economic profile, and proposes several measures to address these faults. Against a continuing trend in which Chester has fallen from a high point of 5th in retail ranking in the UK in 2002 to 35th in 2009, rising unemployment, and an inability to benefit fully from tourism, the ULI panel saw a need for the city to develop a properly co-ordinated and integrated approach to generate economic success. Their perception was that Chester had 'rested on its laurels' while other cities in the region, notably Manchester and Liverpool, had reinvented themselves. Although the panel believed strongly that Chester had huge unrealised potential, it found a culture that was 'caught between over-confidence in the appeal of its formidable but fading assets' and a form of 'conservation paralysis that has seen the city walls crumbling while endless strategies and plans are developed without any over-arching vision to bring them all together effectively'.

This paralysis was attributed in part to physical and institutional fragmentation, confusion over accountability and decision-making, and to divisions among community organisations. Whilst the panel was impressed by the number of groups and people wanting to see Chester develop as a successful city, without a consistent goal or galvanising vision these groups were often seen to be working against one another. Thus whatever the leadership and decision-making structures that are put in places, the challenge will be to develop a strategy that will unite the various groups and organisations behind a single vision to improve Chester's position as a leading economic and cultural centre. As a well respected community body, Chester Civic Trust must clearly take a lead in securing this vital consensus.

As to the vision, the panel felt Chester should focus on being a distinctive regional city with its own brand that exploits its heritage but is not afraid to look forward. Local entrepreneurs, the student community and existing local businesses must all be engaged around creative innovation so that Chester can remain a city with a strong business hub, regardless of competition from Manchester or Liverpool. Heritage alone cannot fulfil the potential that Chester has to re-establish itself as a vibrant centre, but an enterpreneurial approach based on cultural tourism, entertainment and heritage could be a very strong proposition if it brought together all the strands of creative potential within the local business and educational community. Finally, the panel suggested that Chester needs to remember the maxim on which its retail heyday was based, namely 'quality not quantity'. These are strong messages that the city cannot afford to ignore.

In a period of uncertainty, a review of the past 50 years provides valuable lessons for the future. Over the whole of this period the need to strike a balance between respect for the past and acceptance of change has remained the Chester Civic Trust's core principle. But in pursuing its objective of making Chester a better place, it has never retreated into conservatism or negativity. In the 1960s, James Chandler wrote a series of fortnightly articles on behalf of the Trust, which were published in the *Chester Chronicle* and *Cheshire*

Observer under the banner of *Viewpoint*. They are brief, personal and remarkably perceptive. In one he writes about the pitfalls of designing modern buildings in the Georgian style. In another he praises the care that was taken by the City Engineer in the detailing of the ring road, citing for example the roughly textured and 'self-effacing' low crash barriers which, in today's less sensitive climate, have just been replaced by aggressively ugly grey concrete blocks. Walking along the towpath of the Chester Canal, he mused how in future times it might be overhung by three and four storey houses, each with its own private terrace overlooking the water. He foresaw the terraces full of life, with children playing, washing hung out to dry, and pot plants receiving attention. Interspersed amongst the houses he saw pubs and restaurants, the whole served by a network of narrow walkways linked over the water by footbridges. Cars would be superfluous since residents would be within walking distance of work and shops, but small boats might be used on summer evenings. But then, as if waking from a dream, he recalled that this was after all only 1967, and that people still had almost everything to relearn about providing themselves with civilised urban housing. 45 years on, the canal has been largely developed; but looking at what has been achieved, there is still a lot to learn about civilising the city. The Chester Civic Trust's role remains as relevant as ever.■

2010 Celebrating the Trust's Golden Jubilee

A calendar, a gala dinner, a conference, a book, a schools' project, an environmental project, walking tours, special lectures, a family quiz, tea towels and commemorative mugs were just some of the ideas put forward when Stephen Langtree, a Vice President of the Trust, asked how we might celebrate our Golden Jubilee. These 'first thoughts' were presented to the Civic Trust Council in April 2008 and a sub-committee was duly formed, chaired by Stephen, to deliver as many as possible. In the end there were no souvenirs except for a calendar (and this book!) but our legacy project is the splendid 'Four Seasons' mosaic at the entrance to the Roman Gardens which was achieved in partnership with Cheshire West & Chester Council and Chester Renaissance at a cost of approximately £16,000. Many other Jubilee activities ran throughout 2010, leaving just the mosaic (and this book!) to be completed afterwards. It was a very busy year indeed, not least for the enthusiastic members of the Jubilee Committee. Altogether there were over 20 special events or activities tailored to the Jubilee theme – some of which are depicted here. An 'End of Jubilee Party' was held in St Mary's Centre on the Trust's 51st birthday in January 2011 during which the food, wine and accompanying slide show reminded those present of the five continental excursions made by the Trust since 1990. As this book is the very last part of the Jubilee programme It's a good opportunity to thank everyone who helped to make it a most memorable year. ∎

50
Chester Civic Trust
1960 - 2010

Gala Dinner

(Top) The Lord Mayor, Councillor John Ebo presented commemorative plaques to Cyril Morris (left) and James Latham, both founder members of the Trust in 1960.

(Right) Guest speaker, Lucinda Lambton (centre), with Civic Trust members Doreen King and Philip Harrison.

Chairmen (past and present) with the Trust's Vice Presidents (left to right): Peter Bingham, Stephen Langtree, Christine Robinson, David Evans, Graham Fisher, Rosemary Martin, Allan Pullin and James Latham.

Flower Power

The Floral Bed in Grosvenor Park was designed
by Jack Garrett, seen here (left) with David Jones,
Stephen Langtree and John Jones.

Conference Success

As part of the Jubilee programme, Chester Civic Trust hosted a national conference organised by
the Historic Towns Forum (HTF). The event focused on 'The Value of Community Engagement'. The
photograph shows Debbie Dance (Chairman of HTF), Stephen Langtree (Vice President CCT), Chris
Winter (Director HTF) and Tony Barton (Donald Insall Associates, sponsors of the conference).

Schools' Art Project

During the Easter holidays forty pieces of artwork, produced by local school children, were displayed at the Queen's School. Kate Harland, the Council's Learning Development Officer, worked with classes in six local schools, talking about the history, heritage and buildings of Chester and displaying artefacts from the Grosvenor Museum. The exhibition opened with a tea party for the children, their teachers and parents: guests included Councillor Richard Short, the Council's executive member for Culture and Recreation (above left).

AGM

The Trust's AGM was held at Eaton Hall: (left to right) Dr Simon Thurley (Chief Executive English Heritage and guest speaker), The Duke of Westminster (President), Vice Presidents James Latham and Stephen Langtree and the Chairman, David Evans.

Historic Plaques

A launch event marked the completion of the first set of commemorative plaques sponsored by Chester Civic Trust and Cheshire West and Chester Council. The photograph shows Gerard Tighe (left) representing the Chester Guild of Tour Guides and Councillor Hilarie McNae (front) the Council's 'Heritage Champion' with other members of the Historic Plaque team. The plaques celebrate prominent Cestrians and the influence of the Freemen and Guilds.

The 'Four Seasons' Mosaic

Situated at the entrance to the Roman Gardens, the 'Four Seasons' mosaic was a successful partnership between the Civic Trust, the Council and Chester Renaissance. Over half the cost was contributed by Chester Civic Trust including a legacy left to the Trust by Suzie Langtree. The figures in the mosaic represent the seasons of the year interspersed with scenes illustrating Roman gardening and horticulture. The artist who created and executed the design was Gary Drostle. The mosaic was unveiled by The Duke of Westminster, President of Chester Civic Trust.

Chester Civic Trust today

Chester Civic Trust is a voluntary organisation of over 400 members with one interest in common: the conservation and improvement of a unique historic city and its immediate surroundings. The Trust's mission statement is:

"To be the leading local voluntary organisation dedicated to the preservation and improvement of our built environment".

It achieves this by:

- Raising awareness and stimulating public interest in the built environment, buildings and their settings:

- Encouraging and promoting high standards of architecture, urban planning and design:

- Securing the improvement of buildings, sites and streetscapes, that have historic or public interest.

Registered as a charity, Chester Civic Trust relies entirely on the voluntary activity and the skills, expertise and enthusiasm of its members. These individuals have been the Trust's greatest assets throughout the past fifty years, giving their time without payment and united by a willingness to do what they can to maintain and improve the city. Their efforts have given the Trust a powerful voice within the community, arguing for a balanced response to development and change, whilst protecting the existing historic built environment.

Currently 40 members are office holders, members of committees or represent the Trust on other organisations. Since the early years the Trust has maintained a specialist committee structure which has developed and adapted to meet the challenges of each decade. There are five committees and each chairman reports to an elected Council.

The **New Works Committee** examines selected planning applications nearly every week and comments constructively to the local planning authority on behalf of the Trust.

The **Urban Development Committee** was established to achieve a multi-disciplinary approach to urban issues. It deals with: traffic and transport: conservation: strategic planning: open spaces, and regeneration. It aims both to stimulate public interest in the city's built environment and to promote a high standard of urban design.

The **Publicity Committee** publicises and promotes the interests and activities of the Trust. It produces regular Newsletters and advertises lectures and events. A website www.chestercivictrust.org.uk has been created. Members of the committee are also active in writing to the local press and speaking to local organisations.

The **Events Committee** provides a range of services to members, its aims being to involve the whole membership by encouraging them to meet socially and to discuss and debate matters of common interest. It organises visits to other historic towns with similar concerns and

Elected members of the Civic Trust Council (2011-12): back row: - Andrew Pannell, Tony Barton, John Herson, Jean Evans, Stephen Langtree, Peter Cocker, Martin Meredith, front row: - Ann Jones, Ruth Davidson, David Evans (Chairman), Doreen King and Jan Hore, (Absent – Christine Russell, Richard Hale, Peter Hadfield and Martin Bocking).

arranges lecture programmes and talks for members. It also hosts visits by other civic societies and bodies (voluntary, local government, central government, etc). and is involved in community-based activities. For example it participates in the annual Heritage Open Days celebration and has hosted visits by Government Ministers and visitors from other countries.

The **Palace Group** manages the Civic Trust's office in Bishop Lloyd's Palace and is responsible for letting the two large meeting rooms that are available to groups and individuals.

From time to time, special committees have been constituted for specific events, notably in recent years for the Millennium Festival, the New Year Honours and for the Golden Jubilee of the Trust.

Chester Civic Trust is one of the largest and most active amenity societies in Northwest England. Few others, if any, offer such a wide variety of lectures and excursions (including overseas visits) backed by strong technical committees and individual expertise. The Trust helped to set up a regional association of civic trusts and societies, and has always supported the national 'umbrella' organisation, The Civic Trust, now 'Civic Voice'.

That said, the World is changing and the ability of voluntary organisations to attract younger members is a growing concern. Chester Civic Trust cannot rely for ever on any traditional formula; it will need to adapt and change if it is to remain as an effective voice in the community. Hopefully there will always be people who love this city and are prepared to stand up and be counted. ■

Martin Meredith joined the Trust in 1999 specifically to manage the finances of the Millennium Festival. Soon afterwards he joined the Civic Trust Council and has been at the forefront of most administrative roles ever since. He managed the refurbishment of Bishop Lloyd's Palace and then served as Honorary Secretary from 2003-10. Undaunted, Martin is now the Trust's Honorary Treasurer and continues to manage the Palace Group, chair the Events Committee and 'hold the fort' as acting Hon Sec ! In addition, Martin is the Treasurer of Civic Voice, thus ensuring that Chester Civic Trust plays its part in supporting the national civic movement.

© Photo by Terry Latham

CHESTER CIVIC TRUST

is the leading local voluntary organisation influencing the character and quality of our built environment.

Founded in 1960, the Civic Trust remains at the forefront of local environmental issues and is widely respected for its independent and constructive opinions.

We are a registered charity with over 400 members drawn from all walks of life. Our organisation has no political affiliations but, as a non-statutory consultee, enjoys a close working relationship with Cheshire West and Chester Council and Chester Renaissance.

PRESERVATION AND PROGRESS

Chester Civic Trust has been instrumental in the preservation of many historic buildings and in the establishment of the city's conservation areas. While these remain vitally important, we also lobby for high quality modern architecture that respects its surroundings.

Alongside all of this we champion improvements to the public realm, (street surfacing & landscaping), public parks and open spaces, architectural lighting, heritage interpretation, cultural infrastructure and public transport.

CHANGE IS INEVITABLE AND AS A MEMBER OF CHESTER CIVIC TRUST YOU CAN HELP TO SHAPE THE FUTURE.

Founder member of

CIVIC VOICE
talking civic sense

cumbria · lancashire
merseyside · manchester
NW acts
cheshire

North West Association of
Civic Trusts and Societies

Historic Towns Forum

© Photos by Patrick Faleur

Presidents, Chairmen and Honorary Secretaries

PRESIDENTS (Past & Present)

Colonel Gerald Hugh Grosvenor DSO DL
later 4th Duke of Westminster (1961-1967)

Robert George Grosvenor TD JP DL
5th Duke of Westminster (1968-1976)

Gerald Cavendish Grosvenor,
The Earl Grosvenor (1977-1979),
now 6th Duke of Westminster
KG CB CVO OBE TD CD DL (1979 to date)

VICE PRESIDENTS (Past & Present)

* Colonel F C Saxon OBE MC JP (1962 – 1973)

* Mr James Chandler MBE (1969 – 1974)

* Mrs Gertrude Jones JP (1974 – 1993)

Mr A L Wheeler (1975 – 1991)

Mr Gerald Burkinshaw OBE (1979-1983)

Mr Harry Churton (1983 – 1999)

Dr Rosemary Martin JP (1984 to date)

Mr Graham Fisher (1991 to date)

Mr Stephen Langtree MBE (1994 to date)

* Mr James Latham (1999 to date)

(founder members)*

CHAIRMEN (Past & Present)

Colonel F C Saxon (1960 – 1961)

Mr T L Masters (1961 – 1963)

Dr J Quentin Hughes (1963 – 1966)

Mrs Gertrude Jones (1966 – 1971)

Mr Gerald Burkinshaw (1971 – 1975)

Dr Allan V Pullin (1975 – 1978)

Dr Rosemary Martin (1978 – 1981)

Mr John Maddock (1981 – 1985)

Mrs Jackie Leech (1985 – 1987)

Mr Graham Fisher (1987 – 1990)

Mr John Wakeman (1990 – 1991)

Mr Stephen Langtree (1991 – 1994)

Mr Roy Archer (1994 – 1996)

Mr Stephen Langtree (1996 – 2001)

Dr Peter Bingham (2001 – 2004)

Mrs Christine Robinson (2005 – 2008)

Mr David Evans (2008 to date)

HONORARY SECRETARIES

Mr James Chandler (1960 – 1967)

Dr John Tomlinson (1967 – 1969)

Miss E B McIntosh (1969 – 1972)

Miss M Moffat (1972 – 1973)

Mrs M Buchanan (1973)

Mr Brian Lewis (1974 – 1980)

Mr Denys H Goose (1980 – 1984)

Mr Bob Clough-Parker (1985 – 1987)

Mr Stephen Langtree (1987 – 1991)

Mrs Sue Atkinson (1991 – 1993)

Mrs Jan Hore (1994 – 2002)

Mr Martin Meredith (2003 – 2010)

Bibliography

Chester: A Plan for Redevelopment:
Charles Greenwood, Chester City Council, 1945

Chester: a Plan for the Central Area:
Building Design Partnership, 1964

Chester: A Study in Conservation:
Report to the Minister of Housing and Local Government and the
City of Chester by Donald W Insall and Associates, H M S O, 1968

Chester: Conservation in Practice:
D Anne Dennier, Town Planning Review, Vol. 46, No. 4, October 1975

Chester: Conservation Review Study 1976:
D W Insall and C M Morris, Chester City Council

Conservation in Action: Chester's Bridgegate:
D W Insall and Department of the Environment, H M S O, 1982

Conservation in Chester 1986:
D W Insall & C M Morris, Chester City Council, 1988

Chester: The Future of an Historic City:
Building Design Partnership, 1994

Environmental Capacity: A Methodology for Historic Cities:
Arup Economics and Planning, 1995

The Rows of Chester: The Chester Rows Research Project:
Andrew Brown (Editor), English Heritage, 1999

2000 Years of Building: Chester's Architectural Legacy:
Chester Civic Trust (2001)

Chester Civic Trust archives:
Cheshire Record Office

Acknowledgements

This book was conceived by Stephen Langtree, Chairman of Chester Civic Trust's Jubilee Committee.

A book of this kind cannot be produced without the help of many people – members of the Trust, relatives of founders of the Trust and friends of both the Trust and the authors.

Chester Civic Trust is indebted to the authors, Peter de Figueiredo and Cyril Morris, without whose expertise, forbearance and determination to complete the task nothing on this scale would have been possible. Special thanks also go to Jan Hore for research and administrative assistance, Julian Treuherz and John Healey for advice and proof-reading and Caroline Holton for compiling the index. Jean Askew, Patricia Green, Sir Donald Insall, Jackie Smith, Sid Tasker, John Tweed and Eileen Willshaw have also been invaluable for their help and support. All have given of their time freely and willingly in the interests of the Trust.

Many of the photographs were taken by the authors and the editor and other photographers are acknowledged as follows:

- Tony Bocking
- Brecht-Einzig Ltd
- Cheshire West and Chester Council
- Chester Renaissance
- David Cummings
- David Heke
- Gary Drostle
- Tom Hand
- Donald Insall Associates
- Doreen King
- Ian Lawrence
- Don McIntyre
- John Mills Photography Ltd
- Simon Warburton
- John Wolfenden
- Philip Wrightson

Chester Civic Trust also gratefully acknowledges the assistance of the staff of Chester History and Heritage and the volunteer members of the Chester Photographic Survey.

Every effort has been made to contact copyright holders of illustrations reproduced in this publication. Any omissions are inadvertent and will be corrected in future editions.

The map of Chester has been reproduced by kind permission of Marketing Cheshire.

The book was designed and typeset by **de Winter** with particular thanks to Stuart Williams. Printing by ESP Colour Ltd.

Index of names

General index

References to Chester Civic Trust and local authorities are too numerous to be included in the index.

About the Authors...

Peter de Figueiredo trained as an architect and urban designer and has practised in historic building conservation in the northwest of England for over 30 years. He was Head of Conservation and Design for the City of Chester from 1989-99 and an Historic Buildings Inspector for English Heritage from 1999-2007. He is now an Historic Buildings Consultant in private practice.

Peter was President of the Cheshire Society of Architects from 1995-97 and has served on the Cheshire Diocesan Advisory Committee and the Historic Churches Committee for the Roman Catholic Dioceses of Lancaster, Liverpool, Manchester and Shrewsbury. Peter is also active in the Institute of Historic Buildings Conservation and was a member of the Northwest Design Review Panel from 2007-11.

His previous publications include *Cheshire Country Houses, The Victorian Architecture of Manchester and Salford,* and *The Rows of Chester.*

Cyril Morris is a Cestrian, born with in the City Walls. He graduated in architecture and town and country planning, joined the Cheshire County Architect's Department and was appointed Assistant County Architect in 1965. From 1974-89 he was Director of Technical Services for Chester City Council with responsibilities which included the management of the city's internationally acclaimed conservation programme. He initiated the city's Civic Award Scheme and represented the District Councils' Association on the British Tourist Authority's Heritage Committee.

In retirement Cyril has continued to be an active member of Europa Nostra ('The voice of Cultural Heritage in Europe') and Chester Civic Trust (of which he is a founder member). He is a past president of the Cheshire Society of Architects and a past chairman of Chester Magistrates. A trustee of professional and local charities, he has also been an honorary adviser to the Falcon Trust since it was established in 1979.

...and the Editor

Stephen Langtree is a retired chartered civil engineer whose professional career was with international consultants Binnie & Partners and Black & Veatch. After graduating from Manchester University in 1975 he joined the firm's Chester office and worked on many projects involving water supply, flood protection and canal restoration.

In 1986 Stephen joined Chester Civic Trust but declared himself **not** to be a 'committee person'! Within 12 months he had succumbed by joining the Civic Trust Council and becoming the next Honorary Secretary. Thus began a second career, involving countless committees, campaign groups and partnerships. Stephen is now a Vice President of the Trust and, before that, was its longest-serving chairman. He is a director of the Chester Historic Buildings Preservation Trust and an executive member of the Historic Towns Forum. He co-founded Chester in Concert and Art For Art's Sake and was the first chairman of the North West Association of Civic Trust Societies (nw.acts) from 2002-07. In 2011 he was appointed MBE for his 'services to the community in Cheshire'.

Previous publications include co-editing *2000 Years of Building – Chester's Architectural Legacy (CCT, 2001)* and *Conservation Area Awareness (nw.acts, 2009)*.